T0065427

FINDING YOUR
SPIRITUAL HOME

ENOCH MAMO

BALBOA.PRESS
A DIVISION OF HAY HOUSE

Balboa Press books may be ordered through booksellers or by contacting:

Balboa Press
A Division of Hay House
1663 Liberty Drive
Bloomington, IN 47403
www.balboapress.com
844-682-1282

Print information available on the last page.

ISBN: 978-1-9822-5281-6 (sc)
ISBN: 978-1-9822-5283-0 (hc)
ISBN: 978-1-9822-5282-3 (e)

Library of Congress Control Number: 2020914787

Balboa Press rev. date: 10/31/2020

*To my kids Nahom and Nebiat,
my love for you
inspires me to be a better man every
day. I will always love you.*

Contents

Chapter 2: Spiritual Mutation

Chapter 3: Measurement And Perceptions

Chapter 7: Conscious And Subconscious Mind

Chapter 8: Self-Image

Chapter 14: Masters And Slaves

Chapter 15: Opinions And Values

Chapter 16: Forgiviness And Judgement

Introduction

Discovering your spiritual home is understanding the power of choice. It is not circumstance, people, or place, but rather your choices that determine and guide your life. Choice is the difference between people who are broken by situations and those who thrive in the face of adversity. People are often broken by traumatic experiences in their lives, such as divorce, the conflict of war, verbal abuse, physical trauma, emotional upheaval, racism, death of a loved one, financial hardship, disability, or illness. At the same time, you will find people who thrive despite facing the same misfortunes. How?

To live a life of happiness, strength, courage, and gratitude, you must choose these feelings consciously and wisely, in good times and bad. They are not always easy choices, especially in tough times. But the right choices must be made in times of great success, and in times of difficulty.

The consequence of choosing negativity is a life of misery, pain, fear, worry, anxiety, discontent, sadness, perturbation, confusion, shame, regret, guilt, hate, anger, resentment, and vengeance. That is what is on the other side - a life of endless suffering.

If you are waiting until your life is perfect to be happy, courageous, and grateful, there is some bad news. Your life will never be perfect. You could wait your entire life and die without ever being happy. The good news is, you can choose to be happy right now, despite what is going on in your life. It is your choice; it is your life. Every single human being on this earth will have problems or challenges at some time in their life, such as poor health, family problems, marriage issues, financial stress, school, work, politics, wars, famine, anger, fear, guilt, shame, regret, resentment, corruption, deceit, verbal abuse, physical abuse, emotional abuse and more... the list is almost endless.

The best thing you can do is to choose the problems that you want to focus on.

For example, Martin Luther King Jr. chose to fight the social and economic injustice African Americans were facing. Bill Gates chose to fight poverty and disease around the world. The problem you want to focus on does not have to be as lofty as these, but you must consciously choose a problem. When you focus on a chosen problem that offers a financial, spiritual, or emotional reward, you will inadvertently starve your focus from the unchosen problems.

Many chosen problems are made subconsciously due to societal programming, such as buying a house, marrying, having children, and choosing a career. Examples of unchosen problems include health issues, where and when you were born, the death of loved ones, natural calamities and other problems that are outside your control. As you go through the chapters of this book, you will realize the different topics have one underlying theme, and that is choice. The best way to build your spiritual home is by consciously choosing to build the life you want, one brick at a time.

Being at home spiritually means you are living according to the same philosophies and principles every day: serenity, confidence, courage, forgiveness, love, gratitude and peace of mind. You live with no guilt, regrets or shame, whether you are rich or poor, in a state of chaos or calm, in a foreign country or at home, married or single, have good health or sickness, are with or without kids, are in debt or debt-free, in rain or sun shine, you are always at home. Being at home will prevent you from wasting your life in anticipation of the future or regretting mistakes of the past.

The path to spiritual enlightenment is not transcribed step-by-step for you here - nor is this book meant to be a "how-to" of sorts. Rather, use this book as a gentle guide to help you find your spiritual home in your own way. Take in a section or two each day as part of your regular philosophical practice and then consider how the ideas speak to you in your life. Enjoy the process as you journal about what you are learning and reap the rewards from the universe as you incorporate the philosophies into your daily living.

1

Faith & The Present Moment

CLEAR SIGNALS

What kind of signals are you sending into the universe? Are they clear, low vibration, mixed? The universe works with 100 percent precision, just like a printer replicates an exact version of the document in your computer.

Imagine you have an old PA system in your hand and the universe is a big ear sitting just a few yards away. The universe can only hear the signal or messages you are sending. The means by which you send your messages to the universe, or infinite intelligence are through your dwelling thoughts, beliefs, faith, self-image, and perceptions. These are the only means of communication; they are the language that the universe understands.

So, what messages are you sending through these portals? What do you want to say to the universe?

The universe does not care where you are living or about your past, but you make it care by dwelling on those things. Forget about other people, they cannot send messages to the universe on your behalf. Everybody has his or her own receiver - or the universal ear that processes their unique messages or prayers – and only you can choose what you want to say to the universe. You can allow other people, your past, or situations to influence your message. Letting external factors and people determine your message consequently affects who you become and your realities.

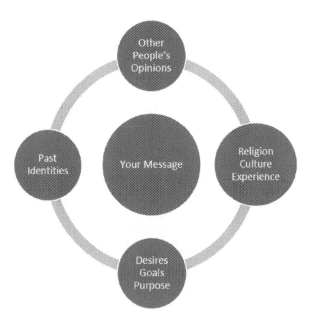

In the above diagram, you can see four sources of influence that can impact a fragmented perception of your self-image and influence your messaging, but there are many more. For example, consider the impact of social media, television shows and news, leisure, friends, finances, and your past failures. You consciously or subconsciously decide which of these things influence what kind of message you are sending to the universe. Remember it is your choice. You can hear opinions, have experiences, and live in those situations, but they have no power to send a single message to the universe on your behalf. All of these things are happening in your environment and you are the only one with the keyboard. Here, faith is communicating your aspirations and dreams to the universe, even though you do not yet see them in your realities or the visible world. Here are some messages you can choose to send:

- Your aspirations, dreams, and prayers
- Your courage or fear
- Your contentment or discontentment
- Positive or negative energies
- Your past identity, including failures, weaknesses, experiences, abuses, mistakes, upbringing, and performances
- Your opinion of others, including judgments and criticisms

- What you were told you can or cannot do and what others have said is possible or not possible for you to achieve
- Old beliefs, dogmas, values, and habits you previously held

In the past, ignorance and old programming made you think that your voice did not matter. You subconsciously added all the noises as part of the message to the universe. You did not know how the universe worked. Now you know it is only your voice and choice that matters. Remember, you are always saying something to the universe, consciously or subconsciously, through your thoughts. Do not send mixed messages to the universe. Be a sweet lover of your prayers or dwelling thoughts. You can choose to ignore your past and other's opinion of you when you are communicating to the universe.

In our nervous system, it is the clear electrical and chemical signals that our neurons carry between each other to turn a potential action into our reality or new habits when repeated over time.

Some action potentials are silenced, while others are transmitted from one neuron to another to empower our thoughts and actions. All these processes happen within you, not externally. You are in charge of choosing which action potential to send from one neuron to another and which ones are supposed to be silenced. With time, repetition and affirmations will strengthen the synapses that will ultimately form our new habits.

HABITS OF VISUAL STIMULATION

Constant stimulation in the visible world often makes it difficult to live in faith or in the invisible world. Living in faith does not have to be difficult, but because we are programmed to react to the physical world, this habit makes us forget the use of our faith. Living in faith is a habit that you regain consciously, by remembering that everything you are witnessing in your visible world was first created in your invisible world through faith. Even though physical stimulation has made us ignore our faith, nothing can take it away. You just forgot to use it and how to use it.

When you immerse an object in water, it will be displaced by the volume of the object immersed. If you live 90 percent of your life reacting to or getting stimulated by physical world, then it means you are living in faith only 10 percent of the time. The best way to live a balanced life, is to see everything in your physical or visible world as an extension of your faith. Everything you see in your invisible world; you will witness in your visible world soon. This is not a denial of reality or the visible world, but it is an acknowledgement of its origin and limitations.

The smallest particles that we are made of are not actually atoms, but fields. Everything in the universe is made of fields, including the mysterious black holes, the stars, the planets, the asteroids, the galaxies, the animals, the sun, the moon, my phone. Everything. Fields are just like the magnetic fields that are not visible to the eyes, but you still observe their effects when two magnets are brought close to each other. That is how faith also works. You cannot see it, but it animates the world. For example, you can see the work and influence of faith in people when they are healed or in miracles, but you can never see faith with your naked eye.

Faith defies science, reality, facts, nature, logic, and human understanding. Faith is seeing what you want to see – all the changes that have already taken place despite what you see in the visible world. It is ignoring your past illusions and the adversities they created for you in the visible world and creating a better world for yourself. Faith brings into existence the non-existent or what does not exist in the visible world, and recognizes the constant changes taking place in your invisible world. You must choose to see what you want to see, and which changes you want in your life. By making these your dwelling thoughts, your subconscious mind will create your new reality. On the other hand, you can continue clinging to your old negative beliefs and thoughts that have created a bad life for you.

The denial of your existing conditions and realities means that you believe in the power of faith and infinite intelligence within you. It means you accept and believe that faith is more powerful than your circumstances and conditions, that the invisible creates the visible. You see, we are basic flesh and spirit, but all other blessings or misfortunes are given to us based on our faith, which is shaped by our right-mindedness or ignorance.

So, FLESH + SPIRIT + (X) FAITH = (X) MAN or (X) WOMAN

The X is the variable here, while flesh and spirit are constant.

The X is the type of faith you have, and that determines the level of your wealth, skills, talents, health, conditions, and realities. The X creates your specific life, lifestyle, and success – both the good and the bad in your life. The X represents all the people living in this world who all have different personal life, realities, and conditions. What is your X?

The people who failed to get out of poverty, suffered poor health or gave in to weakness believed more in the power of their visible realities created by their illusions and ignorance, rather than believing in the power of infinite intelligence within that can create new realities. They remained fixated on one of the changing faces or past ideas or opinions of themselves. They saw themselves as powerless, and believed their destiny and fate was in the hands of other people or was at the mercy of external conditions. They were ignorant of the power of their faith and the infinite intelligence within.

THE SOURCES OF EXTERNAL REALITIES

There are two components of faith, receiving and rejecting. Receiving includes accepting prayers as received and being content while rejecting is saying no to self-limiting thoughts, poverty, worry and deprived self-image. You mut say NO as many times as you say YES. There is defiance in faith and that is the adultery that God encourages.

Understanding this concept of faith improves your life since you use the challenges or scarcities in your visible world as a material or asset to cultivate and strengthen your faith. The candle must melt to give light and the challenges and scarcities in your life are the candles that need to melt to give way to enlightenment. To learn something new, there must first be ignorance. The challenges in your visible world are not only important, but vital in strengthening your faith to achieve success. Do you need faith if everything is good in your life? Definitely not. Living in faith or exercising faith comes as a result of you trying to change something in your life. One of the definitions of faith itself is bringing into existence that does not exist now. So, if everything exists now and your goals have been met, then what do you need faith for? You cannot want to have faith and at the same time hate the conditions that enable you to exercise your faith. Loving the concept of learning new things but hating that you were ignorant is foolishness. To become open to new lessons, we must accept that we do not know everything. Every piece of information we have so far is minimal when you consider what is still out there for us to learn. This drives us to discover new knowledge, to wrestle out of nature's hand new ideas.

The visible world is not the most important because it is the by-product of your invisible creation or faith, so it is already a past manifested. Though you have no power over the past, you do have all the power regarding what you can create now in your invisible world. It is ignorant for anyone to live in weakness when he can live in a place of power. What you are creating in your invisible world will manifest in the future, even though each goal has a different gestation period. If you live in faith, you will reap the harvest of those invisible creations now, in the present moment. If you have no faith, you will wait with the rest of the world for manifestation, which is just a by-product, and you may never live to see that day. But with faith, you get immediate gratification as soon as you accept it, with no waiting and no anxiety. The gratification comes from your acceptance, rather than manifestations. Acceptance is an action you can take because you can decide to accept or reject.

When you focus on the by-product, or the external environment, you are strengthening or reinforcing and perpetuating the false identity of YOU that you created with your illusions and ignorance in the past. The stimulation you get from the by-product will continue to reinforce your old beliefs, self-image, and perceptions. In this case, you are not being proactive, you are living a reactionary life. Rather than using the power of your invisible creation, you let the external environment and the past determine your fate and your happiness. Hence, things will never change for you, since the only way a change can take place is in your invisible world.

If a factory produces defective phone chips, you will not change anything by focusing on the defective chips. You must fix the machines that produce the chips for real change to take place. The external reality or visible reality (by-product) is the chip, while the factory that produces them represents the invisible creation. You must focus on fixing your invisible creation because it is wasteful to focus on what has happened in the past and ignore thousands of defective chips or realities that keep getting churned out from the factory. These by-products could be your poverty, failures, sickness, fear and worry and many more could be added soon if you do not fix the factory (invisible creation). First, stop the production or addition of the defective chips, then accept those defective chips that have been produced and transmute the situation for your own benefit. If a dam breaks and floods a city, you do not only focus on dealing with the resulting damage, you repair the dam or put up a barrier to stop the water from flooding the city again.

In your invisible creation, you should be working in two ways. First, start a new production, and second, stop the current production of defective habits and perceptions.

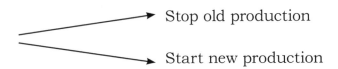

Stop old production

Start new production

Every astronomical success or failure, every unbelievable victory or loss, every mastery or mediocrity, every mind-blowing piece of architecture or mediocre work was once just a thought in someone's mind. It is not chance, guesswork or luck. You are what you create in your invisible world.

THE VISIBLE MANIFESTATIONS

The life you are living now, the people you are interacting with, your work and your situation are all part of your unhidden, or visible, manifestations. The boxes you opened in your life are what you are enjoying now, or not enjoying. But that does not mean this is it. There are an infinite number of boxes waiting to be opened. Many people get stuck on that one box they opened by clinging to their past. Look up and move on, there is a bigger world out there with many unopened boxes waiting to be discovered.

PATIENCE

Patience is acceptance of your prayer as received, while impatience is focusing on why you did not receive what you asked for. While patience, faith and true prayer tells you to accept gifts as received, even when you do not see them in your visible world. Do not focus on the by-products (which also took time to manifest through years of invisible creations programmed by the society and ignorance). New faith and prayers do not manifest new realities overnight. Stop digging out the seeds you planted to see if they are germinating. Every birth in this world has its gestation period. We know it takes a woman's body nine months to prepare for the birth of a baby. Every dream, purpose and goal have a gestation period as well.

Accepting as received does not mean you cut corners, it means whatever you prayed for has taken place in the invisible world, and you must then wait its natural time for it to appear in the visible world. The same can be said for acquiring wealth or changing your attitude and behaviours.

Some things have a short gestation period of just seconds or minutes while others take months or years to manifest. For example, a moment of inspiration or getting healed. And others fall between the two time periods. Conventionally, people call the short gestation periods miracles, but the truth is, even the goals and purposes that have longer gestation periods are miracles as well.

Many people quit following their goals or dreams because they do not understand the concept of gestation period. The best way to stay focused and succeed is to make your actions and steps as divisible as possible. Simplify them to the smallest doable steps - something that you can do every hour or minute in the day. Nature thrives in simplicity, at the microscopic level. It would be also very simple for you to measure your progress to ensure consistency, creativity, and productivity.

CONSEQUENCES ARE OUT OF YOUR HANDS

If you cannot control the consequences, you do not need to have worry, doubt, or fear. Simply focus on what is in your control, which are your thoughts or invisible creations. Then, whatever you dwelled on will become your reality, whether you like it or not and whether you want it or not. Your dwelling thoughts will manifest, just focus on what you control. These are your only powers: conscious thoughts and choices.

If your mind wanders into doubts, this is normal and will disappear over time, they are just the remnants of your past habitual thoughts.

CONVICTIONS

You cannot desire success and think about failure. Conviction gives the seriousness that your dreams and purpose needs. It is the fuel that runs the engines of your dreams and goals. Live by your conviction every day, no matter what you see or hear. The only true reality is in the invisible world.

Having alternative options is just talk, and thoughts of quitting or losing cloud your goals and purpose. If there is no strong purpose or desire to achieve a goal, it should not be even called a goal, it should be called a wish. And a wish is not faith because you believe it may not happen. In faith, you believe whatever you prayed for or desired has already happened (acceptance or recognition) in the invisible world. So, have that conviction in the visible world. Do not talk of time limits, plan B or alternative options.

If you have accepted your goals as if they have happened, then how can you make alternative plans? If you are talking about other plans, it means either you have no faith, or you did not accept your prayers as received.

Enoch Mamo

BAD FAITH

You will never be happy or succeed in life if you keep selling your soul through fear, which is a negative prayer. What you fear will manifest, and your fear will come to pass, causing you to suffer twice in the process. The first suffering is the fear itself and the second suffering is the manifestation of that fear. Let's say you feared losing your job or feared having poor health. Before those things happened, the fear made you suffer, then those things happened, and you suffered again.

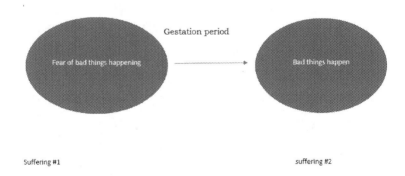

Suffering #1   suffering #2

The gestation period for people who live in fear is a period of suffering, while the gestation period for people who live in faith is a period of courage, gratitude, contentment, happiness, creativity, and imagination. This is choosing faith, even over success. You must think, "If bad things happen, then they will happen. Meanwhile, I will not make myself suffer in their anticipation."

Whenever you allow fear to take over your life, you are killing creativity, happiness, courage, abundance, gratitude, and good health. In each moment there is an opportunity to choose the positive or negative energy. Stop suffering, choose faith and positive energy, and live well.

If you live today fully, wholeheartedly, positively, and in faith and gratitude, then tomorrow will reward you. If today, you make yourself suffer in fear, worry or anxiety, then tomorrow will punish you with more suffering for your bad faith or ingratitude. Have you waited too long to start living? Do what you are supposed to do today and live happily in faith, fortitude, and gratitude. You will never have everything in life, your life will never be perfect. So, learn to celebrate the imperfection. The youth, energy, and health you have today will never come back. True you may have more money or success in the future, but nothing will bring back this day. The only way we overcome the lies and illusion of tomorrow is by enjoying the now, today. Every generation, every human who ever lived and is living now, has all gone through the same passage. Not even the eternal souls, whose names and work will live forever, can come back, and enjoy the days that are gone.

FAITH OR SUCCESS?

What you call progress or success is external, even if you gained it. It can change, be taken away from you, lose its value or go out of fashion. In the end, success is not really yours. But faith is really yours. It is always with you until the end of your life. It does not depend on others or their opinion or external factors and accomplishments. It is yours now, tomorrow, and next year. It is the only real treasure you have. Losing it means you lose everything. You will always be empty, incomplete and a failure if you lose faith. It is better not to succeed than to lose your faith.

HOW THE WOMAN GOT A NEW BODY

I once witnessed a woman get healed by a Christian religious healer. A medical doctor who witnessed this healing confessed that it was medically and scientifically impossible for the woman to talk to the healer while her lungs and windpipe were hooked up to the artificial breathing machines she relied on. Of course, what the doctor meant was it was impossible in the *conventional world* (that only recognizes visible or physical objects and changes). The miracle I witnessed that day could only happen in faith. Just as in quantum physics, by faith, the woman managed to teleport to a healthy version of herself, just as she was able to teleport herself into a sick version of herself in the past, through dwelling thoughts. Here, teleporting refers to a physical transformation through faith, not a physical transportation.

Live consciously, and only focus on what you want to see in your life, and you will also be able to teleport yourself to that existence through faith.

WASTE OF TIME DOUBTING FAITH

Just like wasting your time on negative thoughts or emotions, a lack of faith in God and the infinite abundance and blessing within you also wastes your life. The whole universe itself and life on earth are all forms of miracles, so why would one try to live a life in any other way, when miracles are so exciting and thrilling. The spiritual world is infinite and there is no limit to what you can imagine and discover. To only focus on external treasures allows them to steal away your present moment or life.

PRAYERS

Are you sure that what you prayed is really what is best for you? Desperation is not a form of prayer, but rather a miscreation that overwhelms you with thoughts of scarcity. These eventually become your dwelling thoughts and soon, your reality.

How do you differentiate desperation from normal prayers or dwelling thoughts? Desperation is characterized by fear, worry, perturbation and impatience, while positive dwelling thoughts are characterized by contentment, fortitude, joy, peace of mind, patience, strength, love, and a healthy sense of self-worth.

FAITH IS NOT FOR THE WICKED

Living in faith not for the faint of heart. It is believing in what you do not see, thus, the faint-hearted quickly give up and lose faith because they do not see in the visible world what they believed in. So, they move on to the next thing, their next goal, project, or alternative. Their energy is scattered all over the place, in all directions. They have attention-deficit for faith. But the righteous stay strong in faith, no matter what goes on in their physical or visible world. They are not faint hearted, and they do not give up easily and lose focus. The faithful know that what they create in their invisible world can never fail to manifest. It takes fortitude and boldness to live in faith.

I have never manifested any past realities that I did not already create in my invisible world. That is my incontrovertible proof. I need no more evidence than the reality of my past life. I will only focus and take care of my creations in the invisible world.

We sometimes glorify those who suffered for their cause. We admire them and see them as heroes. But there is no glory in getting arrested, tortured, or killed. What we are celebrating is their determination and commitment.

A negative person does not need a good reason to be fearful, depressed, worried, or unsettled. A negative mind will find the tiniest of excuses to torture himself and have those negatives feelings and thoughts take over. But for the positive minded, nothing will make them have those negative feelings or thoughts. Whether facing death, torture, poverty or any other challenges, many positive thinkers have deliberately put themselves in those positions because of their commitments. For example, people who fought colonization, dictatorship, and racial discrimination.

THE PRESENT MOMENT

MY BEST MOVE IS MY NEXT MOVE

I heard those words in a documentary from a young man who had just been released from prison. These words have a very deep meaning for me as it means living fully in the present moment. Your best move is your next move, no matter if the move is in a positive or negative direction, or if it is small or big. Your next move becomes your best move by mere fact that it is what you are doing in the present moment, which is the most powerful and most precious time of our lives. If you understand the meaning of those words deeply, and experience their truth, then you will realize that you have great power over your life and begin living in the now.

Your next move is your best move and the most powerful move you can make in this world. The past is dead, and the future is not yet real, so the present moment is all you have.

DEAD IN THREE MINUTES

The human body can only survive for about three minutes without oxygen. After just one minute, our brain cells start dying, and in less than two minutes, irreversible brain damage begins. This shows the simplicity and fragility of life that we hold so dear. The things that we cannot live without for even for three minutes is free and abundant and available to us all the time. There is unimaginable beauty and miracle in this simple fact of life. It is true that the best things in life are free. Our lack of appreciation and gratitude for this free essential of life shows how far we have departed from natural laws and nature. Instead we live in disillusions and ignorance, made up by our thinking mind that was programmed by society.

Your every breath should be a breath of gratitude as your life is truly sacred and great. Not because of the big things, but because of small things like oxygen. These three minutes apply to everyone, whether you are a famous inventor, a popular president, a philosopher, or billionaire. This fact is just one way that nature is whispering to us that we are all equal. This simple and mundane everyday occurrence – breathing – helps explain our existence in this universe.

THE PRESENT DAY IS THE MOST IMPORTANT

By now, we understand that the present moment is the most important, both philosophically and spiritually as well as intellectually. But how do you make sure you are not wasting your days doing or thinking irrelevant things? The best thing you can do is to prepare daily goals. Not weekly, monthly, or even yearly goals. Pay more attention to what you do on daily basis. This habit will force you to live in the present moment and to accept and work with what you currently have, rather than thinking about what you would like to have in the future. It will also keep you focused and help you get more out of your days.

Let us suppose you have a farm and you spend your time planting in the morning and harvesting in the evening. If you harvested a small amount every day – say 20 percent – you would not stay in the business of farming very long. If you received 20 percent on any test in school, it would mean a complete fail. So, if you harvested only 20 percent of your capacity or potential as a farmer, then you would have failed, as you would not be able to feed your family or support your financial needs. This is the situation many of us face in life.

What is the use of crying or getting angry at the end of the year, if you have been ignoring the results at the end of each day? The end of year outcome does not matter at all when you have ignored your daily goals. When you focus on the daily outcomes, then you will also have things to celebrate regularly. At the end of each day, you can celebrate your success or adjust and make corrections for improvement the next day. Celebration and improvement are both very important for human enlightenment and growth.

Judge your success by the type of days you are having, not by the quality of your years. It is not the last drop that empties the glass, it is the constant emptying that leaves it void. It is the same for success or failure. The moment you realize success or failure is not the actual moment it happens, as it started happening long before to lead to the current result.

Several days before my daughter turned six years old, she was asking me if her looks or physical features would change on her birthday, since that is when she would become one year older. I assured her that she would not notice any changes, because it is hard to notice the big changes in our lives over hours or days. Big changes are accumulative. It is the everyday effort that people put in that one day leads to a big success. Just the way success is built block by block, failure is also built block by block over time.

Spiritual Mutation

2

DEVELOPMENT OF PERSONALITIES

Spiritual mutation in the process of human development can either produce light mutants evolved to adapt and thrive in society or dark mutants that are maladaptive and detrimental to the individual and the society at large. A single person has multiple mutants in the form of inner personalities. The word persona is a Latin word which means mask. I see the different personalities that exist within us as spiritual mutants or masks that either destroy or enrich our lives. The light mutants are your inner personalities that are enriching your life, while the dark mutants are your inner personalities or malignant spirits that are stealing your happiness, health, and abundance. These stealing mutants can be in form dark desires, hate, relationship breakdowns, addictions, and some physical illnesses. It is a corrupted self-destructive system, that leaves one to live a purposeless life with minimal self-control and awareness. You become a slave to the habits and addictions of the dark mutants. Just like a drug user can steal, beg, prostitute, or kill for his or her addiction, the person living with a dark mutant is controlled by its urges.

While we all adopt and live with many personalities throughout our lives, we are the awareness behind the many personalities or masks we have within us. You are neither the light nor the dark mutant. When you struggle to overcome addictions, negative thoughts, and emotions, it is the awareness who witnesses these decisions and their workings. The awareness is the silent observer, overseeing the hundreds of desires, urges, passions, phobias, fears, worries, excitements, disappointments and struggles you have experienced over the years.

MISUNDERSTANDING ILLNESS

People who are suffering from mental illness are the ones who are generally treated as having negative energy. According to Christian science, evil arises from a misunderstanding of God's reality or goodness of nature, which then leads to incorrect choices. So, the people who many shun and resent as evil or having negative energy, do not have a true understanding and self-awareness. This lack of understanding leads them to completely identify with the malignant spirits or dark mutants that dwell within them. It becomes very hard for the hosts to separate themselves from these dark mutants. It becomes almost impossible for the conscious awareness to truly see what is happening in their lives. I put 'TRULY' here, because the person can only see what is happening in his life through the perspective of the malignant spirit, not his or her awareness. As such, the person has distorted views of their reality, and this misunderstanding leads to bad choices in thoughts, emotions, actions, and responses.

Many people with personality disorders are wrongly portrayed as selfish and manipulative, but we forget that they are suffering from chronic emptiness and emotional turmoil because of the dark mutant or malignant spirit that is controlling them. Persons with mental illnesses are sometimes perceived by the public to be in control of their disabilities and responsible for causing them.

A narcissist or a person with bipolar disorder is not a king seated at his throne, trying to cause suffering to other people, but rather a soul being tortured by the demons that he cannot control. When you understand, you will see them as people who need our love, understanding and forgiveness most.

DANGEROUS URGES OF THE DARK MUTANTS

A very good example of where we can witness the extremely dangerous urges of a dark personality is the case of the 74-year-old DeAngelo, a serial killer and burglar in California in 1970s and early 1980s.

After his arrest on April 24, 2018, DeAngelo was recorded talking to an inner personality named "Jerry" that had forced him to commit the heinous crimes.

While sitting alone in a police interrogation room, DeAngelo said to himself, "I did all that, I didn't have the strength to push him out. He made me. He went with me. It was like in my head, I mean, he's a part of me. I didn't want to do those things. I pushed Jerry out and had a happy life. I did all those things. I destroyed all their lives. So now I've got to pay the price."

Here we observe the confession of the light mutant in him, confessing the crimes of the dark mutant, or dark inner personality - while his awareness witnesses the conversation.

Most people do not have dark personalities that make them commit burglary, rape, murder, or other serious crimes, but many of us live with some mild forms of dark personalities or mutants that bring unnecessary pain and suffering to our lives. These mild dark mutants can lead to depression, self-harm, or suicide in the worst cases. A lot of attention is not given to them because they are not often harmful to society as a while, but rather to the family and friends of the individual.

The following are some of the features of these dark mutants:

- Dark mutants can be explained in the same way as malignant cells, viruses, or bacteria. Just like a virus or bacteria, the dark mutant adapts and becomes part of your personality. Just like the viruses or bacteria pose as one of your normal cells to evade detection and elimination, the dark mutant also does everything to avoid detection or its elimination. When it becomes 'you' or part of you, then it is easy for it to survive, and you will do anything to protect it. Just like any other organisms, it wants to ensure its survival by any means. In the case of malignant cells, they possess mechanisms that allow them to evade the immune system's surveillance and identification as "non-self."

- The dark mutant will completely block you from seeing other people's perspective, pain, suffering (manifestations of their own dark mutants). It is always right, and the other person is always wrong. It will tell you, "you see what they did, or you see what they are doing to you?" When you see things or problems from the perspective of the dark mutant, you will only see the problems in other people. It will absolve itself from any kind of responsibilities or wrong doings. That ensures its survival. Even seeing the other person as a problem is not enough, you will still feel anger, resentment, bitterness, and vengeance. You will continue keeping the score sheet to write down the sins, weaknesses, or mistakes of the other person. When you are blinded from seeing another person's pain or perspective, you will not even notice your own cruelty.

- Sometimes we can see the dark mutants in the urges that lead us into irrational fears, panic, actions, and thoughts.

- Desperation for love and respect from other people confirms the presence of dark mutants in us. You grow very resentful and angry if you believe you are not getting the love and respect you deserve from other people. So, you try to coerce the other person into respecting and loving you. You believe someone is in possession of what you highly value. So, you are under the control of someone else's opinions, words, and actions. The control button, or switch of your self-worth, self-image, peace, and happiness is in someone else's hand. You are switched on and off at will. When you do not have control over your life like that, you are very weak and vulnerable. To compensate for your weakness and loss of control, you become aggressive and resentful. You should not blame the other person; you are the one who gave away your control.

- Unyielding sense of hurt and inability to forgive people who we perceive have hurt us. Sometimes, you come up with rational and convincing reasons why you should forget the hurt and forgive the other person, and you feel it is the right thing to do. But the hurt and resentment will not go away. This is because those thoughts are outside our conscious awareness. It is our unconscious mind that is manifesting the psychic pain.

THE HIGHER PURPOSE

There are higher purposes that we serve piously, that are controlling our lives.

These are either:

A. The dark mutants: ignorance, or evil spirits

B. The light mutants: wisdom, or the spirit of God

These two higher purposes are the sources of your thoughts, actions, emotions, and motivations. Instead of trying to deal with millions of manifestations, it is better to deal with the source. Consciously choose the light mutant and align all your thoughts, actions, and motivation with it. While bad habits are seen as a failure by society, they are a success for the dark mutant (for which you are fulfilling its urges). What is a loss to one side is actually a win for the other.

Each temptation you overcome is a win for the light mutant, which builds your power (self-control) and shifts your alignment. When your egoistic identity or the dark mutant is hurt, it is an indication of where your ignorance and weaknesses lie, so you must correct it. The mental disability created by ignorance is very real, it is the source of all evil in the world.

Wandering away of the mind is not a mutant, however, this is just a fleeting thought. A person with light mutant can have negative thoughts or wandering away of the mind and vice versa. Can you only have dark or light mutants? Yes. Can you have mix of dark and light mutants? Yes, you can have them in different proportions. We spend our energy and time living according to the urges of the mutants we serve. Just as a biological genetic mutation is the source of all genetic variation, what differentiates us are the spiritual mutants we serve; we can literally die or kill for them, because we think they are us. The player thinks he is one of the characters in the game.

If you are playing a video game, you cannot see yourself as one of the characters, just because that character is a hero and reject the role of a villain. This happens when people see themselves as the roles they are playing, rather than the awareness behind the roles. You cannot say, "I am not that dark mutant, but I am the light mutant." You are neither. These are just inner personalities that have grown into habits and roles.

THE HOUSE OF WORSHIP

If you went to an Ethiopian Orthodox church, you would likely see people kissing the ground, the doors, and the walls of the church as they came in for worship. You would not expect to see such rituals in Catholic or Pentecostal churches. In fact, you would be surprised to see anyone doing that. Muslims also have different rituals and ways of praying. Similarly, when you are under the influence or control of different mutants, whether dark or light mutants, you live your life according to the characteristics, urges, needs and values of that mutant. For example, if you are serving the victimhood mutant, then it is expected that you will whine, blame, become weak, feel anxious, depressed, resentful, and bitter. Your creativity, productivity and happiness will also decrease because of those emotions and thoughts. Just like places of worship, you should not be surprised to see someone manifesting those feelings, because he is serving the victimhood mutant. Anybody who had served the same mutants you had, would have ended up just like you and would have had the same life you did.

You should starve and defund the dark mutant, because the demon depends on your money and hard work for its survival. It also depends on your mental energy and time to propagate its fears, anxiety, depravity, and wretchedness. You should start cutting off all the resources that were strengthening this demon that has been wasting your life.

CAN YOU TALK TO HATE OR IGNORANCE?

Can you talk to hate, ignorance, resentment, or jealousy? Some people's faculties are completely ruled by the feelings generated by their dark mutants. How can you ask someone who is being controlled by those feelings to overcome them? They have just become the slaves or agents of the devil, and do not have the freedom to make independent decisions. The dark mutants decide for them and influence their decisions. The wrong approach is getting fixated on the name and physical identities of the person who is carrying those feelings. That is focusing on the wrong enemy, because the real enemy is the dark mutant.

Similarly, when you focus on your past identity, you are focusing on the wrong enemy. The real enemies are the self-limiting thoughts, fears, worries, anxieties, and other thoughts produced by the dark mutants within you. Do not give those feelings an identity of any kind, otherwise, you will end up creating a permanent identity out of your flaws. The labels and identities given by psychologists are one of the major hinderances to healing.

In a personal relationship or even at work, you can have the dark mutants predominantly talking to each other. That is what people commonly refer to, when they say, "you bring out the best or the worst in me." In the case of bringing out the worst in you, this is when someone constantly focuses on your weaknesses or mistakes. It is the cause of many arguments and resentments in relationships. In terms of Jungian Psychological Types, this is a case where two subconscious inferior functions are dealing with each other. We have to learn to speak to the light mutants in people in order to bring out the best in them.

Sometimes, however, it is you who brings out the worst in yourself by communicating with the dark mutants within you. Some of these dark mutants have been with you since childhood, and you may not have the cognitive ability to identify the mutants, or you are living in denial of their existence. Therefore, the dark mutants dominate your decision-making, thoughts, and actions. You consult your insecurity or negative self-image when making decisions. Unless your mindset changes, your circumstances will not change.

If, in the past, you have been communicating with other people's dark mutants (their anger, hate, jealousy, and so on), you are accustomed to talking and working with them, and perceiving them as powerful spirits that can hurt you. Now, you can see their true colours. To the person within whom they dwell, they bring suffering, scarcity, and savagery. Is this what you were trying to reason with or argue with? Is this who you considered your enemy? Is this what you were trying to blame for making you a victim or hurting you? Is this what you are trying to payback in kind? Understand what you are dealing with and you will have infinite love and forgiveness.

IN A BAD RELATIONSHIP?

The only way you can know whether you are being controlled or influenced by dark mutants is by the feelings and interactions you have with those you are in relationships with. If you are filled with bitterness, hate, resentment, irritation, blame, anger, and vengeance, then you know they are coming from the dark mutants in you - not from the other person. Is that the state of mind you want to have when dealing with people in your life? You will suffer and you will make them suffer, too. Nobody wins, no matter what the other person does. The dark mutant is clever at focusing the attention on the weakness of the other person while your worst pain is coming from your own negative emotions and thoughts. These are the true logs in your eyes. Once you overcome those negative feelings and the enslavement, your perception about the other person's weakness, mistakes and the hurt you are feeling will completely change. It will be replaced with one of love, forgiveness and understanding. Look within for the answers, not at the other person's opinion, action or words. Use the pain and the negative thoughts as an alarm that awakes you into correcting your misunderstandings.

HOW DO YOU EXPECT THE DISEASE
TO TREAT YOU DIFFERENTLY?

How do you expect a disease to treat you different from anyone else? An illness brings pain, suffering, poverty, scarcity, discontentment, sadness, anger, hate, unforgiveness, abuse, conflicts, and tears families apart. How can you hold a grudge against an illness? Ignorance, which is the biggest cause of mental illness, leads you and other people to make bad decisions and cause hurt and pain to each other – but what else do you expect from the illness? Just as illnesses such as cancer, malaria, meningitis, and diabetes cause damage to our bodies, mental illness causes damage to our physical and mental health, our relationships, and our wealth. If a person loses a limb or his hearing ability, his memory or mental faculty because of an illness, would you blame him or her? Similarly, because of mental illness, would you blame a person if they lost their temper, family, career, or finances? It is all part of the manifestation or symptom of an illness, just like the lost limbs or other impairments caused by physical ailments. How can you allow the illness to destroy not only the life of the sick person, but also your life? How can you allow it to destroy your peace, love, forgiveness and abundance? Come back to God. Do you expect cancer, Alzheimer's, dementia, or multiple sclerosis to manifest into better performance or better health? Of course not. It is the same for mental illness – it manifests in negative ways in all aspects of our lives.

Nobody in this world chooses to be sick or ignorant – but somehow sickness and ignorance choose you. Have sympathy, empathy and understanding for the people who have gone through, or are going through, terrible manifestations. They did not choose to have or experience what they are going through. Otherwise, they would have chosen far less harmful or painful manifestations.

SELF-ABSORBED MUTANTS

Expertise in understanding the properties of a matter makes you a scientist. In other words, you understand the interactions and reactions of the different elements' atoms and nuclei, their transformations, their potential, properties, use, dangers, and patterns. This understanding helps produce an almost infinite number of products that enrich our lives. Similarly, the understanding of human emotions, spirit, motivations, actions and behavioural patterns, enables us to live in peace with other people. If we are not self-absorbed in our egoistic identities, we will understand other people and therefore love and forgive them.

Measurement And Perceptions

3

TRAPPED BY VIEWS

I once watched a YouTube video of a monkey trapped in a fishing net. The monkey tried hard to free itself, but it was all in vain. Even another monkey tried to help, but also failed. A few minutes later, a man came and simply lifted the net and the monkey was free. That is what learning the natural laws can do to your life. Only in this case, your soul or spirit is trapped by fear, shame, worry, anxiety, negative self-image, self-limiting thoughts, guilt, regrets, hate and anger. One after another, the knowledge and application of natural laws lifts up the net that entraps you and your happiness. Abundance, creativity, peace of mind, good health and courage will be released into your life and the world.

What we call wisdom is mostly how we interpret the world around us. Our eyes see everything inverted.

When the image reaches our brain, it adjusts the image so that we can see it upright. That is the first and most basic form of interpretation. The others are not so obvious. We must use a mixture of gained wisdom and natural instincts to interpret them. Our interpretation here is biased on opinions of others or what we learned from the society (the original sins).

Most of us miss out on the blessings of life because we were looking for wealth in poverty, investigating our shortcomings and failures. You cannot find light in the darkness no matter how hard you try. Move on from thinking about poverty and scarcity all the time and think instead of wealth and abundance. Your perception is more important than the actual external conditions.

Do you know people who say, "I eat very little, but I still gain weight"? And, as expected, they gain weight? What you choose to see will become your reality.

WHAT DO YOU SEE?

If you see yourself in a certain way, whether it is having or lacking certain qualities or characters, then it is not the presence or the absence of those things that matter, but whether you see yourself as having them or not. Even what the world sees in you does not matter. It is your perception of yourself that is important. For example, if you say to yourself, "I am not good with this or that," then your perceptions will begin creating your reality. It is a question of, what do you see?

When it comes to seeing other people, look for the positives. No matter how nice someone is to you, it will never be good enough for you because the ability to be happy about another person's actions or behaviors, only lies in you. You are the only one who can create that peace within yourself. In the past, you may have chosen to focus on the person's weakness or negative sides. To free yourself, you must focus on his or her divinity.

How can there be any unforgivable man or woman? Isn't all journey a movement towards love, forgiveness, and healing? All is a movement towards the source, becoming light again. I cannot hate myself. And if I am wise, I cannot hate others. We arrive at enlightenment by going through past pain, selfishness, failure, fear, and confusion. They are the markings and scars on our journey in life.

CONFUSING AND FEARFUL SITUATIONS

When you are afraid of something, you feel like you are in a sticky and confusing situation. Remember it is not the situation that is really producing these feelings, it is your mind or illusions that are producing these situations. The feelings are coming from within, rather than from the situations themselves. You bring what is inside you to a situation or event. If a situation intimidates and unsettles you, do not blame anyone or anything else. Instead, look within and tell yourself it is not the situation that is making you feel this way, but your perception of it.

For example, if you are intimidating by coding, remember it is not the coding that is hard or confusing, (as even 5 to 7-year-olds can be really good at it). It is your mind producing those feelings based on opinions and past experiences. Children do not usually have that negative baggage from the past.

Your every thought, action and response to a situation reflects your mental status or attitude and your perception. If you are full of fear and confusion, then those feelings will come out in whatever situation you find yourself in. If you are courageous and confident, any situation will bring out those qualities out of you. That is why you will find different people have different reactions to the same situation. The different situations are like different hands that squeeze an orange. The same juice will always come out, no matter the hand that squeezes it. Likewise, the same man will come out of different situations.

This is good news for all, because you do not have to worry about how to react to different situations. Instead, work on what is constant - your constitution: your attitude, thoughts, perceptions, and emotions. Do not try to cover the whole earth to avoid the thorns, just cover your own feet, by having a clear and firm constitution or principles.

Be in control of your situations and moments. Be confident and tower over them. Do not be belittled or disconcerted by them. Both danger and power lie in you. There is the danger that you could become poor, or homeless. There is the danger that you could lose your mind, become unhappy or weak, hateful, angry, fearful, vengeful or anxious.

You also have power and intelligence in you, that can make you wealthy, confident, happy, and courageous. You can become creative, loving, forgiving, caring, calm and strong.

Life is not about waiting to receive all the best things to become the best person, it is about making the best out of your current circumstances or situations.

Do not wait for the perfect conditions, skills, environment, or circumstances to come your way. You do not have two lives; you have one life. So, treat all your circumstances as an opportunity to have a great life and do great things. Do not become a slave of your environment.

FOCUS ON WHAT YOU GIVE

Focus on what you give rather than what you receive from others or the world. Your prayer should be asking what you can give, not only asking to receive. Many people are worried about what they can receive from others or the world, hence face a lot of anxiety and disappointments. When you are consciously aware that what you receive is directly related to what you give, then you will no longer feel that worry and stress. So, give as much as you want and as much as you can. When you think in terms of giving, rather than receiving, then the stress will be replaced by joy and passion, because you can share what you love with other people. You will be giving what made you happy, strong, abundant, and loving. When you focus on receiving or taking, you live in fear, worry, anxiety, doubt, scarcity, and frustration. In the end, your life is about giving. You even give your body back to the earth - transforming from one form of life to another through birth and death.

DIFFERENT LEVELS OF PROBLEMS

Sometimes we create problems out of things that are not important to us and invite problems into our lives by accident. For example, you start smoking, drinking, or doing drugs and then you become addicted, which becomes a major challenge to overcome.

Important questions to ask yourself when dealing with a problem are, "Why am I dealing with this problem? Does overcoming or solving this problem improve my life? How can I benefit either financially, emotionally or spiritually from solving this problem?" You need to decide what victory looks like to you.

Perhaps you are struggling to learn French, but you do not know if you will gain financially from it, or what you will do with the knowledge. You must ask yourself, "Why am I doing this?"

Similarly, we sometimes create a mountain out of a grain of sand by taking trivial issues and making them into overwhelming problems in our lives. That mountain is only visible to us, but not to other people. Then you are surprised when others do not understand the heartache and misery your problem is causing. How could they?

Enoch Mamo

IT IS NOT THE DOG THAT CHANGES

If you have a fear of dogs, you must understand that you are only facing your own self (the false self, or the ego.) It is not the dog that changes, but you, when you overcome the fear. You can extrapolate this same line of thinking to other areas of your life. When you are facing poverty, you are facing your own self-image of depravity and scarcity.

Many people wait for things or people to change them. That is like waiting for a dog to change, rather than changing your fear of the dog. A dog will always be a dog. There is nothing new about divorce, struggles and failures. They have existed for as long as the existence of human beings. The important thing is how you let these events affect you or shape your life. Some people will use everything in their lives to grow stronger, while others will let situations break them. How you perceive everything in your life is important in determining your success. Whether you like it or not, you are the source of your poverty or wealth, success or failure, misery, or joy. They are all controlled by you, whether consciously or subconsciously. When you are facing them, you are only facing your perceptions of them.

THE DOG CHARGES

Experts advise you do not run when a dog charges at you, but for most of us, our instinct tells us to run. This instinct is programmed from childhood, so it takes a lot of conscious effort and training not to run. For many people, the expert advice sounds counter-intuitive. It is the same for many philosophical ideas or natural laws. Take forgiveness, for example. Why are we sometimes encouraged to forgive someone who did something bad? Instinct tells us to avenge, hate, and maintain resentment for that person. But the natural laws and wisdom asks us to unconditionally forgive, and even love the other person. Why? Because if you do not forgive and choose to hate instead, you are the one who suffers, not the offender. So, it then becomes double suffering - first from the offending person's actions and words, and second, from the hate, resentment and anger that is in you. The latter is the worse form of suffering.

There are other examples of natural laws and philosophies that sound counter- intuitive. It is only in times of fear that you use courage (so fear brings out confidence and courage, and fear is the source.) Ignorance and imperfect knowledge are the sources of wisdom and learning. It is our past weakness that fuels our power and strength. And finally, it is when you are feeling down, defeated, and facing hardship that you need God most.

EMOTIONS AND PERCEPTIONS, NOT PEOPLE OR THINGS

Negative emotions and thoughts can waste your life and make you miserable, and you may blame other people or events for making you take in the negative poison. But regardless, it is the poison that is killing you in the end. Today, it could be this man and tomorrow it could be that woman who is making you drink the poison (making you angry, resentful, or miserable). Today, you are blaming public institutions, tomorrow it could be your material poverty. Your problems are the negative perception and emotions you associate with those things. Do not focus on or waste your life and energy on the fake problems.

The fake enemy or problems are people and situations. The real problems are your negative thoughts, perceptions, and emotions. While you were shooting your arrows at the fake enemy, the real enemy was getting stronger and fiercer by consuming your life and energy. The good news is, while your fake problems are almost endless, your real problems are just a few and very specific. So, if you focus on those, you can overcome them.

If you catch a cold or flu from someone, will you fight the person who passed it on to you? Or you will fight or treat the flu? But when it comes to emotional flu such as anger, hate, vengeance, resentment, guilt and hurt, we fight the person who gave those feelings to us instead of the disease or the real enemy inside. We waste our life and energy fighting the fake enemy while we allow the real enemy to grow and become stronger within us. We then become weak and get enslaved by others. Anger and resentment are signs of weakness.

BUFFALOS AND LIONS

What if a buffalo wished that he did not live in the same place as a lion because the lion is a predator that kills him? Is that possible? No, because buffalos often live in the same areas as lions. Human beings also live with other animals whom we slaughter, as do cheetahs with gazelles, wild beasts with crocodiles, and seals with sharks. Every organism or living thing in this world lives with another living organism that kills or consumes it, and benefits from its demise in some way.

We all live in a world with negative, abusive, and ignorant people. They consume our energy, time, happiness, creativity, and health - if we allow them. The biggest ignorance here is questioning the existence of others. We cannot even question the existence of viruses and bacteria that cause millions of diseases and deaths. If you question the existence of negative influences around you, it is like the buffalo complaining about the existence of lions.

ATTACKING THE IMAGE THAT YOU CREATED

Attacks come from bad judgement and intolerance. An egoistic view that anybody who thinks or acts different should not be tolerated is the same as the buffalo asking why the lions want to eat them. Be more tolerant. We are all God's children. You may have created this bad image of someone who does not act or think like you, and then attacked that image, which was your own creation in the first place.

The reverse is also true. Some people create a bad mental projection of you, and they attack that image. Imagine someone created a hologram of you and gave it negative traits, and then attacked the hologram because of those traits they projected onto it. You know it is not really you, nor are the projections a true representation of you. So, why bother defending the hologram or worry what the other person is calling it? It is not in your power to control what the person imagines, or their mental projections.

THE TONGUE KILLS

It is sometimes said that the human tongue is sharper than a bone, that it can inflict stab wounds worse than a knife. We ascribed to this organ an immense power that it does not have. This power of the tongue, created by myths and ignorance, has made many its prisoner and slave. There is a great temple of fear for this organ, which gives it great power. You often fear what you hate, and you hate what you fear. If you believe that a tongue is that powerful, then any attack becomes fatal to your spirit and self-worth. The moment you realize you are the one who gave the tongue that power, you become free from its bondage. If you gave it the power, you can also take away its power and see it for what it is: a powerless and harmless organ, made of soft flesh that helps us in digestion and produce sounds. Those sounds are completely powerless and valueless if you wish to see them as such. You are the only one who can choose what values to give to the organ and the sounds it produces. What other powerless weapons are you allowing to hurt you?

Enoch Mamo

LIFE'S JUNK HABITS

A friend of mine missed five days of work once because he was having a lot of pain in his knees caused by gout. This happened after he ate a lot of beef at a party, and even took some home to eat later. At the time, I advised him not to eat a lot of red meat because he has diabetes, blood pressure and gout, but he did not listen. He brought the pain on himself and suffered the consequences. We do the same spiritually when we nurse the pain and illnesses we bring on ourselves.

People who are in a habit of eating junk food all time are tricked by their tongues into believing they are doing something good for themselves. Their mind is programmed in such a way that those self-destructive habits are seen as something positive. But this lack of awareness can lead to illness brought on by their lifestyle. The same can be said for excessive drinking, smoking, the use of illegal drugs, consuming too much news or social media, or a lifestyle lacking in exercise. These habits can leave a person in bad health, which can lead to negative outcomes. No system or challenges can defeat a man or woman who has not defeated himself or herself.

VALUES

If you live according to the laws you value, your life will be based on the laws you value. It is not the laws you read about or you were taught that determine the outcome of your life, it is the laws that you value and live according to that will reveal who you are.

You can pray for something, but when your life and actions are contrary to your prayers, it is a confused, chaotic, and unaligned life of misery, desolation, and torture. When you pray for "A" but you live according to "B", the outcome will never be good. No matter who you are, your family background, networks, education, level of intelligence, skills, or qualifications, you will end up in failure and misery.

GIFT VERSES VICTORY

Self-control is a gift. It is not something you strive to achieve or something to overcome, as wrongfully stated in the Tao Te Ching, which posits "victory over self is the greatest victory." This perception puts you in conflict with yourself since you are trying to overcome yourself, thus you will have a struggle that persists throughout your life. But when you see self-control as a gift, a power that you already have, then the choice will be to ignore it or use it. No struggling to get what you have. The philosophy of mind control is a gift and tells you that you are already in attendance at God's party. This is also the only logical and sensible explanation for how millions of people have been able to create abundant lives with astronomical wealth. They were able to subconsciously control and direct their lives to create the life they wanted. Their outcomes show that they all inherently had the gift to control and direct their minds, which is a gift that every single human being on this earth has - the power to choose self-control or run your life on auto-pilot.

NEVER GET CAUGHT AGAIN BY THE NET

When a fisherman throws his net into the sea, some fish get caught and become his meal while others are caught for sale. These fish have life and family just like us. All animals have evolved for millions of years to evade death, whether it be by camouflage, adaptation to feeding habits and evading predators. Even the tiniest plants, animals and organisms want to live, and have developed survival techniques over millions of years to avoid death. Viruses and bacteria mutate to avoid death, not necessarily to cause harm to humans.

As for human beings, we normally get caught by the net of anger, vengeance, hate, resentment and other negative and self-limiting thoughts. But just like a fish getting caught in a net means nothing to the universe, your getting caught or eventual death is not a big loss to the universe. Time will not stop just because a watch got damaged, or its battery died, life will go on, with or without you.

THE GODESSES OF HAPPINESS

The four main Goddesses of happiness are serotonin, dopamine, oxytocin, and endorphin. These are neurochemicals produced naturally in our brain. Many people pay a lot of money to reproduce these Goddesses, through travel to foreign countries, taking drugs or indulging in unhealthy leisure activities. But they are free, as are the most precious things in life. People have set very high prices for the release of the Goddesses. They believe they will get them by having a big house and expensive cars, the perfect family or fame. They forget that the Goddesses are priceless, they asked for none of those things. When you learn to seduce them by simply looking within yourself, they are going to shower you with happiness all your life.

Societal Programming

"YOU" AND THE PROGRAMMING

What you have been thinking as "you" is just the self image and identities you have that have been programmed by society, your experiences and perceptions. The way you think, behave, act, react, eat and talk are all part of the programming playing out (it is simply a program running within you) - just like a robot is programmed to operate in a certain way. But very few people get the opportunity to awaken or learn about these programs. When you awaken, all your ways of thinking and acting, along with your behaviour and your perceptions, will change. You will never be the same person again. The natural laws and the truth shall set you free from this old programming.

What I have learned, is that by "unlearning" these programs, I allow myself to learn new programs. I do this every day by doing something that challenges and changes my old perceptions or definition of who I thought I was.

When you reach certain level of enlightenment, you will realize the interactions between the programmer and the program. The programmer is the observer or the higher intelligence, the program is your thoughts or perceptions, self-image, and habits that shape your actions and reactions. Your body is just an entity that houses the program or the software, like computer hardware. Your ability to separate these two will bring great clarity into your life. You will find that as the programmed, there is no one to blame or get mad at, not even yourself for your past actions, behaviours, and perceptions. When you recognize your role as the programmer, then you can easily remove the corrupt or bad programs from your being.

The program shapes your interactions and successes, your health and career choices, who you are to people, your view of the world, and the by-products or external realities that other people see. This is what most people dwell on and what they understand about life. So, why is it so difficult to change or remove the old programs? This happens when the programmer believes he is the program, or when the observer believes that he is part of the program. It's similar to when you are playing a video game, and you begin to feel as if you are part of one of the characters in the game. But when the observer discerns the two, then it becomes easy to change or remove programs. This is also true in the case of dark inner personalities or the light mutants I discussed in another chapter of this book.

You can see this failure to make the distinction when you look at your past programing as a young boy or girl, and the new programming you adopted through enlightenment or wisdom. Let's say the old programming is "A" and the new programming created by enlightenment is "B". This was how the old programming was created for some people:

- Uneducated parents
- Abusive parents or guardians
- Corrupt institutions
- Bully bosses
- Outdated beliefs
- Ignorant and negative people with self-limiting thoughts
- Tough upbringing with messages of worthlessness as a child
- Negligence by the parents, with no material, social or emotional support

All of the above, as well as other environmental conditions, create or code your old program. But through education, life's lessons, reading books and other spiritual leadership, you can become enlightened to delete the old program and upload the new program on the same entity or person, just like a CPU.

Just like forgiveness, this can seem counterintuitive for some people. But if you reject the old perceptions and immerse yourself into adapting the new programs guided by wisdom, you can change your life in a profound way.

It is useless trying to change or to worry about your habits and behaviours without changing your programs or software first. Displaying or adopting a new behaviour or habits without changing the underlying program is like painting the river. The colour won't stick, and the new behaviour will be very temporary – like an actor who adopts a character for a short period of time. Soon you will go back to your old behaviour and habits. In order to fundamentally and permanently change your behaviour and habits, you must change your programs or software.

MUSIC VIDEOS AND MOVIES

When you watch Beyoncé's music video, "Lion King," it does not matter if you are watching on a VCR, DVD, phone, tablet, PC or laptop. It will be the same music video. It is not as if the song will change because you changed the device on which you are watching it. That is how programming works here. Just like a poison does not care in whose body it is, the damage will be the same. The shape of the body does not matter, nor does the gender, race, past, environment or voice. Running the same program will manifest itself into the same outcome.

Emotions and thoughts such as hate, fear, worry, anxiety, anger and jealousy will destroy any entity (body) they get into, no matter who that person is. It does not matter if that person is Obama or Steve Jobs, because these entities are just like the VCR, CD/DVD. The outcome does not depend on the entity as the program works the same way in every body. Do not allow anybody or anything to program you in that way, whether it is family, friends, parents, siblings, bosses, your career, or pursuit of financial success. If you allow that, you will separate from God and nothing good will come out of it.

THE BAD PROGRAM

Many people have become slaves to their bad habits and addiction such that, they are already weakened and vulnerable to become other people's slaves. It is like in a war. The enemy does aerial bombardment to soften the target in preparation of a ground assault.

You have already been weakened by your bad habits and addictions (a bad marriage or relationship will weaken you in the same manner). No enemy or misfortunes can defeat a man who has not already defeated himself. Sometimes this weakening is done by yourself to yourself whenever you attack yourself through guilt, shame, regrets, and other forms of negative thoughts.

That is how most people become slaves of the system and institutions. When the system beats you, it is because it found a man or a woman who has already beaten himself or herself.

The other cause of softening or weakening is your ignorance or failure to live according to the natural laws. Instead of having principles or living according to the laws, you end up becoming a servant to someone who is living according to them. The software or the programming is supreme. It is always about who has better software, as the robot is only as good as the software or programming operating it.

There are so many robots with different physical features, colours, and faces, but what matters most is the software running it. Just like your face, physical features and name are all nothing. They are just part of the physical robot/entity - the shell to hold the software.

You must also regularly update your software to stay ahead of the game. Do not let anything or anyone corrupt your system. It is your responsibility to maintain and protect its integrity.

SKIN DEEP PHILOSOPHY

We are so used to thinking of ourselves as this or that face, with this colour of skin, and this kind of hair. Our weight and other physical features define us. We do not pause often enough to think of what lies beneath these physical features.

I became more aware of the organism or entity that I am, when I began to think of myself as a vessel - made up of organs, blood vessels, muscles, bones, tissues, and nerves. All of these systems working in synchrony to enable my movement and functions. This organism I inhabit is mainly kept alive by the air I breathe, as long as the oxygen reaches the trillions of cells within my body, I am alive. The movements, survival and health of this entity is controlled by my beliefs, faith, and perceptions.

Some keep their bodies healthy, while others destroy it with bad diet, drugs, smoking and lack of exercise. The entity is controlled by the conscious mind. All the entity asks of you is to keep it healthy. It does not ask for fame, money or expensive things. The entity does not recognize its own identity and name you have given it. The entity must be amused at this obsession you have with its external features. What if without faces, only the entities moved around and interacted? There would be no black or white, no ugly or beautiful faces. Everybody would look the same.

I once saw a monkey in the zoo, who seemed to be curious about all of the people walking by and staring at her. She looked at them as if wondering, "What is this all about?" I see her as an entity as well, with blood running through her veins, her heart beating, her stomach digesting food, her muscular and nervous systems helping her move around. She is just another entity like us, with slightly different features and mental development.

We are so much more than our face or our covers. The entity is composed of the octillion pieces of living, intelligent microorganisms. They are at your disposal to do or achieve infinite things in this life. Make use of them and make the right choices.

BURNING CHEMICALS

I watched an experiment where different burning chemicals emitted different colours of flames.

Each unique color of the rainbow of flames was a signature of the burning chemical. This is the same when it comes to our lives. Our programming and perceptions reveal who we are in terms of our life, work, level of success, happiness, and health. We sometimes think it happens by chance, but each thought and action are part of the formula (chemical component) that gives the flame its colour. Every single action is sacred, whether it is done consciously or subconsciously. Pay attention to them. The universe is more faithful than you can ever imagine.

THE POWER OF VALUE

Many people feel powerless because they either gave up or ignored their values and instead followed the values set by society. Or perhaps their power to create and give value was taken away from them subconsciously. For these people, society set the rules about what is important or useless, what is good or bad, what is respectable or not respectable and what to fear or not to fear. When your own value is not important, then you are not important. When you do not value and respect yourself or your time, value your career choice or purpose in life, then you have lost your saltiness, or value system. Life will throw you out and leave you trampled on the ground because you dimmed the light of the infinite intelligence within you.

The purpose of my life and my philosophical and spiritual work needs not be valued by anyone but me. Only then will the rest of the world also find value in it. That is how you create your value. If you see no good in yourself, the world will see no good in you. If you look at yourself and what you see is a deprived person, then the world can only see a deprived person who is a liability to himself and others. If you see your work as useless or meaningless, the world cannot give it a meaning. If you see yourself or your life as a failure, the world will only see a failed person.

If you think you are a creative person who is doing things that are changing your life and the world, then you will always see time as the most precious gift. If you are just passing through life, then you will have little or no value for time. For example, if you live to only enjoy the weekends, you are wasting five days a week of your life. Why not live a full life every day, 100 percent of the time? The changemakers in the world create the greatest inventions and art, music, movies, and sports because they are living 100 percent of their lives. The utilization of their time leads them to achieve great things and live a great life, and you can, too.

HER FEET WERE STUCK TO THE FLOOR

I once watched a hypnotist hypnotize high school students, and in one situation, the hypnotist told a girl that her feet were firmly glued to the floor. This false and absurd suggestion had a powerful impact on her, such that she could not move or lift her feet up from the ground. She tried hard, but she could not. She even sat on the floor and tried pulling her legs up from the floor, but still they were stuck. This shows the power of suggestion, whether it comes from yourself or others' opinions. Just like the girl, many of us are in a societal hypnotic trance, believing the suggestions of others or our own self-limiting thoughts that are based on illusions.

We give ourselves identities and self-limiting thoughts by referencing past events, experiences, and others' suggestions. We then live the whole of our lives as products of those opinions and identities. As it turns out, we buy into the suggestions given to us, just like the girl, and the illusions become our reality. We even see it difficult to believe there is any other reality.

Break out of this sepulchre, get out and start living your true potential. You have infinite intelligence within you. There is literally nothing in this world that you cannot achieve if your mind can conceive it. Forget the words of the hypnotist, forget the indoctrination.

You see, it was not the struggling that resulted in her freedom, it was the simple and powerful suggestion of the hypnotist that ultimately freed her feet. It does not matter how much you struggle to reform your old self-limiting thoughts. All it takes is the simple realization that all your past self-limiting thoughts, perceptions and identities are illusions of the false "you." You must firmly reject those past identities as they have nothing to do with you. They were distorted and absurd suggestions to begin with, made to a person who was in a deep societal hypnotic trance.

In another episode of hypnosis, I watched the hypnotist tell the high school students that they were Martians. They immediately believed the hypnotist and began communicating in a strange language. He told them a piece of paper towel was a gold certificate and again, they believed him and started fighting over it. This is similar to the way religions, schools, TV programs, popular cultures, fashion styles and social media have all indoctrinated us into believing certain things are important. We waste our lives trying to live according to those values and opinions and we measure and value ourselves based on those material things. Then, if we fail to measure up, we feel worthless.

These are the illusions that are created out of those values and opinions that have been set by others. It is like the hypnotist telling us what we should or should not do in our lives, what we should or should not value, what we should or should not fear. These illusions have dominated our lives since our childhood, such that we are completely separated from the infinite intelligence within and from the truth of who we are and the natural laws.

What if every person's reality is simply a prolonged hypnosis? I remember watching Howie Mandel, the comedian from America's Got Talent, get hypnotized by one of the performers on the show. Howie lived in a different reality for those few minutes, such that he overcame his phobia of shaking people's hands without a glove on. In those few minutes of hypnosis, he forgot about his phobia and shook the hands of the contestant without gloves. His reality had been altered.

Many people are also living in a prolonged hypnotic trance or herd mentality, due to our dominant thoughts. As a result of autosuggestions and hetero suggestions, we received constant affirmations that leave us in a state of hypnosis, not for minutes, but for our entire life.

Conditioning by hypnosis is much more profound and far reaching because it affects a whole race, country, religion or gender. It is what mental slavery, stereotyping and other forms of discrimination are made of. The followers of all the despicably corrupt televangelists are not stupid people, these followers were hypnotized from childhood into believing what they believe, they grew up in that environment, bombarded with that same information just like their parents had been. This environment formed their beliefs, priorities, faith, moral precepts, values, lifestyle, mental and social boundaries. These individuals can be highly educated but still be totally naive and foolishly follow their dishonest pastors or televangelists. They are slaves or captives of their upbringing.

THE CROPS AND THE WEEDS

Everyday we have thousands of ideas. For simplicity's sake, I have grouped these ideas into two groups: The Crops and The Weeds. The Crops are those thoughts and ideas that are in line with your beliefs, principles, constitutions, and faith. So, when these thoughts come to your mind, you should consciously give them more attention and time as they are good and constructive.

Not all the thoughts we have in a day are good, however, and we will often have some that are not in line with our beliefs, principles, or faith. I call these thoughts The Weeds. Most of The Weeds are from old programming from our lives, which we should learn to consciously ignore and move away from. Do not dwell on The Weeds or ask questions about why you are having them. The Weeds will always be there, as no person is perfect, but if you do not care for them and simply ignore them, they will wilt and die. The more time and care you give The Crops, the more starved The Weeds become. This is the only way to overcome The Weeds. Trying to fight, analyze or kill them will only waste your time and energy. Just starve the weeds and deprive them of the care you were giving them.

For example, let us suppose your principle is to love, forgive and stay calm, but you are often disquieted and have thoughts of hate or vengeance. Simply ignore The Weeds and consciously dwell on your principle of love, forgiveness, and serenity. Do not feel guilty for having the negative thoughts. Instead, as you are trying to forgive and love others, give that same love and forgiveness to yourself. Do the same in the case of other thoughts that are in line with your principles, such as thoughts of abundance, courage, good health, poise, and happiness. Dwell on those, and not their opposites.

5

Natural Laws

THE SCIENCE BEHIND THEM

Natural laws are the principles that explain the immutable harmony that exists between the physical and spiritual world. These laws are not manmade, rather, we discover them through keen observation of our interactions with other people, animals, and objects. The recognition of these observable repeated patterns reveals the underlying laws that govern those interactions. Natural laws include faith, love, gratitude, forgiveness, courage and more.

Do you observe the stars, how they are arranged? To the average person, we do not think much about their positions or constellations, and when we witness a storm break a dam and flood a city, we do not understand how it happened to come to that area. But a scientist does. He can track the storm's formation, movements, and landings. He can explain how it was created, its direction and other warnings.

In life as well, most people just witness events or outcomes, but cannot explain how they were created or their movements into their current place in your life. Philosophers, spiritual leaders and sages study failures, hate, fear, frustrations, scarcity, stress, illness, and other hardships to give incisive explanations of how they are created, their patterns and the laws that govern them. This understanding allows for awareness and enlightenment, so one can consciously create a good life and become the master of their own fate and destiny.

Just as a doctor would tell you your illness is likely caused by a certain bacteria or virus, a philosopher, sage or spiritual leader can discern the causes of your hate or love, fear or courage, abundance or scarcity.

Consider this. About 150 years ago, doctors could not explain or prevent the high maternal deaths due to childbed fever. Then one day, Dr. Ignaz Semmelweis discovered it was because the doctors were not washing their hands between surgeries and autopsy dissections and delivery rooms. The maternal deaths greatly reduced when the doctors began washing and disinfecting their hands between procedures. Surprisingly, Dr. Semmelweis' ideas were not accepted by all medical professionals nor his colleagues at the time. These days, it is standard practice that every doctor practices hand washing before performing deliveries and any other surgery.

Similarly, a day will also come when philosophy and natural laws become widely accepted and begin to play greater roles in shaping our society.

Understanding the natural laws will not take you to heaven but will help you to maximize your potential and make the best of your life. Not understanding or following natural laws will make you live in the disharmony of an unprincipled life. Natural laws are very impartial and fair, they are good all the time, to everyone. To those people who ignore them or are ignorant of them, the laws look unfair and cruel, because those people may find the need to blame someone or something for their failures and miserable life.

Some people pray, beg, meditate, affirm, fast, and unreservedly devote themselves to God to manifest what they want in life. They ignorantly believe that the hardships and long years of ascetic life will make them feel worthy of God's grace. They believe they have paid the necessary price to deserve what they prayed for. They believe the success of their prayer depends on the level of their devotion to God, the number of years they prayed, the level of hardship they endured, the length and frequency of meditations they practised, how innocent, harmless and holy they are, how many books of religion, spiritualism and philosophy they have read, or the amount of time they dedicated to their God, spiritual journey or philosophy. But these people forget the most important thing: the natural laws. They ignore the need to live according to the laws and then wonder why they are not receiving what they prayed for. You can punch in the wrong code a million times; it will not unlock your blessings. No matter who is putting in the code or doing the programming, the correct code will get you the outcome you desire. This is regardless of your prayers, skin color, background, holiness, spiritualism, philosophy, or religion. And this is the same for living according to the natural laws: you get what you put in.

PRECISION OF THE LAWS

I am amazed at the precision of our physical world: the way machines work, how planes fly, how the big ships sail, even how my car works. Knowing these systems function with great synchronization, what makes one think that the spiritual world is haphazard; a guesswork or a matter of chance?

Imagine the complexity in the body of a bird, for example. Inside, you will find the muscles, tissues, blood vessels and organs all meticulously arranged to enable the bird's flight. The bird does not fly by chance. In the same way, your destiny does not happen by chance, either. I know my life has been perfectly and precisely arranged according to my faith, whether that faith is guided by wisdom or ignorance or whether it is guided consciously or unconsciously.

Everything that goes on in your life now is arranged according to your faith. Sometimes you have no idea how faith manifests your goals into reality. You may think your life is very different from what you thought your faith was going to bring. For example, you might have thought your dream of becoming successful and serving humanity would manifest in a certain way. You may have believed that if you were faithful, for example, you would first marry the perfect wife, then get a well-paying job, never experience any health issues, and then you would start serving your community.

But the goal of serving your community may be reached by way of a different journey. A different manner of arrangement that is precise and unique to you in your life. The journey you follow to your goal may not look the same as another's. Many people become overwhelmed by doubt because their path is unique from other people's paths, and they give up on their faith, ending up where they did not want to be in life. To get to your goal, you may have to go through divorce, failures, and bad health. You may not believe this is a typical path to success or service to humanity. But in the end, your faith will indeed manifest and you will get to your goal, even if the road to get there was not what you expected. Stick to your faith, stay on course. What you create in your invisible world will never fail to manifest.

The spiritually immature believe that life is ruled by fate or guesswork. Just like my daughter used to guess the words by looking at the images when I asked her to read when she was a child, the spiritually immature go through life unsure, confused and in doubt. They have no strong foundation; they are easily swept in any direction by events, circumstances, or people. Even when they are laying down the bricks, they are not sure of what kind of house they are going to build, they are unsure of what victory looks like. The wise know that the best way to create a good future is done by creating a good plan. They do not believe in chaos; they know harmony rules the universe.

When a student studies hard for exams, for example, and repeatedly goes over the same material, what is he or she doing? He or she wants to get it right, understand the laws or logic, cause and effects and order. It means the student is consciously trying to learn the laws or logics and is ignoring all the illogical or guesswork ideas. Two plus two equals four. While that is the only correct answer, there are an infinite number of incorrect answers. That is what happens in guesswork or chaos. So, in your life too, you must be methodical and scientific in your approach, and understand the underlying laws and patterns.

Your lack of understanding, ignorance, or imperfect knowledge does not mean the world is ruled by chaos. As my daughter soon learnt to read, she came to understand that the seemingly chaotically arranged letters form specific words. That is how life and everything in the entire universe appear for those who do not understand it. Do not be hard on yourself if you have imperfect knowledge or ignorance, just have an open mind and try to learn every day.

BENDING THE LAWS

The spirit maintains the body, what kind of spirit is living in your body or entity? Billions of entities or human beings come and go, moving through the various life cycles and then die, but none of them live outside the natural laws and all of them have unique programs or software. Nobody ever bent the natural laws and lived straight because if you try to bend the laws, you live in suffering, misery, and scarcity.

Generations and billions of people over thousands of years have lived under these natural laws whether they liked it or not, whether they knew it or not, whether they lived according them consciously or not. I am no different. My entity or body can be different, but the laws govern my entire life.

THE PUZZLE

Imagine a man's face made up of the pieces of a puzzle, except all of the pieces were assembled incorrectly. For example, in the place of the eye, the ear was placed. The face would be totally unrecognizable. If your life has not fallen into place, this is what you have in your hand. A puzzle that has been assembled incorrectly. Your ignorance makes you think that life is a guesswork or chaos. That was how you have been thinking all your life. That is how most of us live spiritually, in chaos. What we want out of life and what we do are different. We want good things in our lives, but the things we do are stealing away our energy. Even in your failure, you must still be the master of your destiny. Do not leave your life to fate, guesswork or chaos. Even the smallest of particles or actions in life have meaning, have impacts. That is what all of the laws, properties of water and other elements teach us - that it is not by chance water becomes liquid, solid or gas. It is heated or cooled to certain degrees to get the water to each specific form or status. For a man or a woman, the combination of certain beliefs, faith, perception, and action leads him or her to have a specific status or role in this life. What is heating you up or cooling you down? You may subconsciously find yourself in a certain status, but it is not guesswork that got you there. These programs, laws or components are very faithful. I am not here, in this position or status by chance.

THE GUITAR

I have an acoustic guitar at home and when I play the guitar with my children, we are just strumming the strings incoherently and the sound it produces is not exactly music, or even very pleasant to the ear. But if you give the same guitar to a good guitar player, he or she will produce beautiful sounds and music. What is the difference? The experts know the rules, the pace and the notes. They do not guess.

Likewise, an enlightened person will use their life to create something beautiful and amazing.

If you continue to insist on playing your guitar chaotically (living your life chaotically based on past programming, perception, beliefs, or false sense of self), the outcome is guaranteed: a chaotic sound. A life of misery, bitterness, failure, bad health, and scarcity. Is this how you wish to live, simply because that is how you were living in the past? Live your life according to the natural laws because no musical instrument played haphazardly produces beautiful music. Give rhythm to your life, learn the beauty of celestial symphony.

KNOWLEDGE OF THE LAWS GIVES US CONFIDENCE

Knowing the laws of physics, biology or chemistry gives us confidence to do amazing things. Imagine the task making inanimate objects such as planes fly through the sky. These big, heavy tubes of steel do not fall out of the sky because of natural laws. We use the same laws to create life-saving vaccines and cures for many illnesses. The knowledge of laws and the use of them can lead to discoveries that make the world a better place. Knowledge + usage = power. It is the same when it comes to philosophical and natural laws. Any life lived outside the laws is chaos.

Understanding the natural laws and patterns comes with infinite benefits to humanity, as they are the core foundation of our civilization and its survival. They are the source of everything. The laws make the strong out of the weak, a brave out of the coward, a genius out of the ignorant, a wealthy person out of the poor and vise versa.

The criminals of natural laws are rarely punished by the secular laws, instead the punishment they receive is in form of poverty, misery, regret, guilt, shame, confusion, perturbation, doubt, fear, bad health, scarcity, deprived self-image and wretchedness. It is a complete waste of life and a liability to the world and humanity.

TRUSTING THE LAWS

Why do the planes fly and smaller objects such as my shoes cannot? Because of the laws of aerodynamics (the forces of flight such as lift, thrust, drag, and weight, the Bernoulli Principle, and Newton's first and third laws of motion). We trust these laws; hence, we fly on planes with little worry. But many of us do not trust the universal laws that govern our lives and so we live in confusion and uncertainty. In Bill Gates' documentary, "Inside Bill's Mind," highly intelligent inventors solved some of the world's most challenging problems, such as eradicating polio, improving sanitation systems and creating safer nuclear plants. What gave these people the confidence and ability to solve these problems? The laws. The natural laws gave them the confidence and ability to solve these complex problems. They understood the physics, the chemistry, and the biological laws necessary to produce safer nuclear reactors and more efficient, safer, and cleaner ways of disposing and recycling human waste. They learned how to cure the world from polio and solve even bigger and more complex problems.

There is no other way out of your problem, other than understanding and strictly following the infallible natural laws. There are no short cuts. The laws are very clear and easy to understand. The difficulty lies in the ability of people to immerse themselves and live according to the laws. Easy to break, easy to follow, it all depends on you.

Your true power, freedom, strength, peace of mind, abundance and companionship lies in living according to the natural laws. That is how you enhance and make the infinite intelligence within you work for you (the trillions of infinitely intelligent micro-organisms within you) that have been adopting for survival and success for billions of years. Otherwise, if they work against you, you will live a life of misery. Take care of them and they will take care of you.

Every day, there are a lot of temptations that lead you to act or react according to your past or old programming. When dealing with people or tough situations, you want to go back to your default programming and try to break the natural laws, rather than consciously making better choices. Sometimes in the short run, thinking, acting, or reacting according to your old programming feels rewarding or like the right decision. You may tell yourself, "Just in this one case, I will break the laws and I will act or react different next time." Maybe there is no next time for you. Whenever you break the universal laws, there are serious and very painful consequences. Remember, "killing time" is also a form of breaking the natural laws.

IMPERSONALITY OF THE UNIVERSAL LAWS

Natural laws are good all the time, and all the time natural laws are good. Let us take my car as an example. It does not matter who drives this car, because the engine, transmission and electrical systems would run the same way. It will take the driver from point "A" to point "B," no matter who that person is or what they plan to do at their destination. Whether the driver is off to cause harm or do good, the car will not refuse to run, whether the person has a good heart or bad intention. That is the same for natural laws. They will unfailingly work whether you are following them consciously or unconsciously, whether you are ignorant or wise, rich or poor, a king or a beggar. The universal laws work for everyone the same way, as they are unbiased. That is why, you cannot blame anything or anyone for your failures or success. It all happens according to how you live.

I cannot bend the natural laws; Rather, I must straighten and realign myself according the laws, just as water takes the shape of the container it is in. I cannot change how the laws of faith and gratitude or courage work. I must live according to the them. It is easier for me to jump up and start flying by defying the laws of gravity than break the natural laws and live a good life.

The universal laws are fair and just for each person. Bad faith (guided by ignorance) gives you a bad life. Likewise, good faith (guided by wisdom) gives you a good life. Every person gets the reward of his choice and faith. Mass murderers like Hitler, Mussolini, King Leopold, Stalin, and other dictators were rewarded according to their faith. They became very powerful people who used their power for destruction, corruption, and to attack other races. This proves that these powerful dictators were not made by people (not even their parents or relatives or the environment), they were made by their own faith. People cannot make other people successful or fail. Each person is the master of his or her fate and destiny. You decide your saltiness, not people. If people can control other people's destiny or fate, individuals like Hitler, Mussolini or Stalin would have been thwarted. These people were self-made, just like everybody else. So, the universal laws are fair to you (your faith creates your destiny and fate) even if what is created may not be fair or good for other people.

The universal laws are blind. They will equally work for the sinner as well as the holy, for the weak and the powerful, for the illiterate and the educated, the wicked and the righteous. I do not follow the universal laws because I am a nice person or because I am passionate about them. I follow because I want to have a fulfilling, abundant and happy life on this

Earth. The laws cannot be broken, I can only break myself by not following them. The laws continue with or without me, in rain or shine - whether I am a pastor, philosopher, painter, musician, writer, medical doctor, architect, or drug dealer. No matter where I live or work, what kind of situation I am currently in, the natural laws will work in the same manner and with the same outcome in each case. They are the most comforting and consistent laws in this world.

Why people who break the natural laws are not punished by the secular laws in the conventional world? Because they are slaves and servants to other people. That is why you face resistance and disapproval when you start changing from servitude to being a free man or woman and a master of your life. Masters do not let go of their slaves easily; the slaves must fight for freedom. But there may be a price. You must destroy the "good" boy or girl image and attitude, ways of thinking and habits. Along the way, on the journey of fighting for your freedom, you may offend some people and let others go, but it is all worth it. Always, treat yourself and everyone according to the natural laws.

THE VEHICLE

The natural laws form the spiritual vehicle that will take you to your destination or goals. If the engine, transmission, or the wheels are not working properly, then you will not reach your destination. The laws are not a destination in themselves, the goals are what you want to achieve by using the natural laws. Faith, courage, gratitude, and forgiveness are not goals. Rather, you have faith that something will happen to you, you have courage to live according to this or that. To be grateful, you mention or affirm what you want to be grateful for, rather than offering an empty "thank you."

ENDING THE CHAOS

If a country breaks its secular laws or constitution for bad people, and the laws are upheld for good people who follow the law, then there are no laws. There will be chaos and loss of identity, power, prosperity, and stability. When you uphold the natural laws and your personal principles in some cases but break them in other cases, then you have no personal principles and you are not following the natural laws. You will always live in chaos. Constitutions stand strong over hundreds of years and for hundreds of generations and billions of lives. Different people, different circumstances and different civilizations and eras are guided by the same set of principles and philosophies of a country. That is how you should live your life, under the guidance of natural laws and personal principles.

THE PERMUTATION

The foundation for everything in this world is composed of a few, very basic elements, ideas, or symbols. It is the combination and permutation of the core elements that results in the infinite manifestations. For example:

- Every single word in the English language is written in a different permutation of the alphabet letters A through Z.
- Every organism in the world is made up of carbon, hydrogen, nitrogen, oxygen, phosphorous and sulphur elements.
- Everything in the universe is made of about 90 elements in the periodic table.
- In physics, there are four fundamental interactions/forces known to exist; the gravitational and electromagnetic interactions, and the strong and weak interactions which produce forces at sub-atomic distances and govern nuclear interactions.

- Every figure in the Hindu-Arabic numeral system is made from the symbols 0 through 9.

- In philosophy, I believe the core principles are love/hate, wisdom/ignorance, faith (belief) or lack of belief, gratitude, or ingratitude.

If I had to choose, I would choose those four dichotomies. They are not opposites, but rather lie on different ends of the same scale.

6

Content And Discontent

IF YOU THINK WHAT YOU HAVE IS NOT ENOUGH

In your life, you have everything you think you have, and in exact proportion to how much you think you have. This includes talents, leadership skills, health, and happiness. Remember, it is not you WILL have these, it is you DO have these things.

If you think today about how much you will have in the future, your future abundance will only be assured if you maintain those same persistent thought frequencies over time. Your thoughts today only affect your reality and abundance for today. This applies to perceptions, mental dwellings, level of contentment, gratitude, happiness, poise, courage, and wisdom. These thoughts are the first stage of creation or invisible creation, so they affect your current reality in many ways. Eventually your perceptions and faith will manifest into your external reality in the form of financial wealth, health, and other areas.

If you constantly tell yourself you do not have enough, how will you ever have enough? Where will it come from? The abundance and blessings will only go to those who say they do have enough. Nothing in this world can help a poor man who has a poor self-image and self-limiting thoughts, just as nothing can stop a man who thinks he has enough, who has a positive self-image and thoughts of abundance. As long as you think and believe that the causes of your poverty or ills lie outside of you, then nothing will change in your life.

There is infinite abundance in the external world, but if you do not believe you have enough you cannot access it, even with hard work or desperation. You must change your perception, beliefs, self-talk, self-image before anything else can change. Your lack or scarcity is caused by spiritual discontent.

If you always compare yourself to others, you are not loving yourself. It is ungrateful to believe someone is happier than you, more successful than you, had a better day than you or has a better job than you, because there is infinite intelligence and treasures within you. The "poor me" words and beliefs do not diminish the grace of God or his infinite abundance, but they do diminish your life and make you miserable and poor. This is not loving yourself. You will not progress in life with such a deprived self-image?

The deprived picture you have of yourself is a curse you brought upon yourself. Be loving and bless yourself, as God holds nothing back from you. Change how you see yourself and your conditions and all the blessings and abundance will come into your life.

DISCONTENT IS SPIRITUAL

People misconceive that discontent is a physical or material issue, but often the problem is spiritual. All of your scarcities are caused by spiritual discontentment, such as self-doubt and self-limiting thoughts. Similarly, all abundance, success, great achievements, good health, astronomical talents, love, happiness, come from spiritual contentment.

The work of the conscious mind is to simply make a choice of contentment or discontentment. It may sound easy, but choice is the most important stage of the creation process - even more important than manifestation. You do not and cannot control manifestation anyway, since it is outside the realm of what the conscious mind can do.

For example, if you choose to jump from the balcony of a high-rise building, the injury you sustain is not up to you – but the choice of whether to jump or not is yours. So, it is important to pay attention to what you are choosing to say to yourself. The thoughts and self-image you project will become your reality soon.

THE MEASUREMENT PROBLEM

The way in which you measure can actually change what you are measuring. If you measure a problem, then you will always see a problem. The difference is only in the level of the problem.

For example, if you are measuring the length of a snake (which in this example represents problems), you would proclaim the length of the snake is a certain number of meters and centimeters. When you measure the length of sugar cane (here it represents the solution, abundance, or success), you would say, the sugar cane is a certain number of meters or centimeters. You are simply giving numerical values to what you are measuring, no matter its size. Stop measuring only problems and start measuring solutions and success. Do not dwell on measuring what you do not want to see in your life nor anything that does not benefit you. Focus instead on measuring what you want to manifest in your life. Likewise, do not dwell on measuring the weaknesses of others, for you will manifest those weaknesses and negativities in your own life. What you feared will come true and you will only see the weaknesses that you focused on in those people.

Many people waste time talking about problems, without taking steps in trying to solve them. After spending a long time talking about your tribulations, you become very good at explaining them and giving convincing excuses as to why you failed or how you became a victim. In most cases, you place blame on other people, or external influences such as the environment, your network, your past or your upbringing. Over time, you completely convince yourself that your failures or poverty are because someone or something else, and you spend your time looking for "you see?" moments in your day to confirm your beliefs.

If you have a problem, take time every day to work on it. There are hundreds of opportunities in each hour and thousands of opportunities a day to think of solutions. There are lightbulbs within you, waiting to be lit up. Just like Thomas Edison, keep trying and eventually one of your solutions is going to solve your problem – but whining and complaining will not.

People all over the world overcome extreme challenges and thrive, despite their physical, mental, or emotional hurdles. For example, I once saw a story about a man with multiple sclerosis overcome his physical limitations by writing a book using his nose. His determination was inspiring. With his entire body paralyzed, he could have believed himself to be a victim, and had the best excuse in the world to do nothing. But instead he chose to thrive in life. Rain or shine, we should accomplish what we set out to do, no matter the challenges that present themselves in our lives.

WHAT DO YOU DO WITH OTHER PEOPLE'S PROBLEMS?

Sometimes we dwell on judging other people's weaknesses, rather than focusing on our own, despite there being no benefit to ourselves in doing so. Solving a problems costs time and mental energy, which are both finite precious resources in our lives. Once they are gone, they are gone. So, if you are going to focus on solving a problem, look to solve the problems in your own life first.

We are sometimes defined by our problems or challenges. While some are consumed and defined by the petty challenges in their lives, others are defined by the big problems they solved, such as creating new technologies, going to Mars, or fighting climate change. If you are going to take on someone else's problems, focus on those that benefit you and humanity.

CONTENT-BASED CONTENTMENT

The adage "money can't buy happiness" is true. It is not the amount of wealth you have that determines your happiness, rather it is the contentment or gratitude you have in your life. Your place of birth, your family, your education or career or marital status do not determine your happiness. You can only find satisfaction, happiness, and gratitude in your own mind.

Be conscious of the standards or boundaries you set to receive satisfaction. This can be an endless pit of goals that are impossible to achieve. It is like a drug addict in search of a bigger and better high. Even harder drugs do not produce the satisfaction he craves, leading him to worse cravings and harder drugs. It is a vicious cycle that can waste and destroy your life.

For example, my friend is a smoker and spends more than $400 a month on cigarettes – nearly 25 percent of his monthly earnings. He is not happy about his habit and its financial cost, nor the cost to his health and impact on his wife and children. Though he is an intelligent man, but he is not the one in control anymore. His cravings control him and his smoking budget. In these cases, it is not about what his rational mind wants, it is what his craving wants. Be careful of what you give yourself to as many things can waste your life and money, even the cravings for success, wealth, fame, the search for perfect life, perfect marriage, or perfect peace.

So how can we free ourselves from these cravings? Be grateful and content with your life. Show gratitude for whatever you have, whatever it is. Because if you are not satisfied with what you have now, you will never be satisfied with what you will have, even once you achieve the success, wealth or achievements you thought would make you happy.

POOR USE OF RESOURCES

It is not lack of resources that makes people poor or ignorant, it is the misuse of resources. It is the misuse of your intelligence, time and energy on negative thoughts and emotions. The wise and enlightened know how to use their time and energy to create great technological advances in the world, in the areas of communication, transportation or health care. They spend their intellectual resources working on new scientific discoveries in physics, biology, chemistry, psychology, philosophy, music, and literature.

Economic gaps are created not by a difference in intellect, time, or energy, they are created by the lack of using those resources. No one will benefit from focusing on the negatives or tearing each other down.

I once watched a short video where two monkeys in separate cages were served vegetables. The researcher began by serving both monkeys the same vegetable, and they were both content and happy. Later, the researcher began serving just one monkey a different vegetable, while the other received the original vegetable. The monkey who did not receive the new vegetable became increasingly angry and frustrated, even throwing his vegetables back at the researcher and shaking the cage door with anger. The other monkey began getting stressed as well, from witnessing his friend's frustration. We can take two very important lessons from observing these behaviours.

1. Our anger, frustrations, stress and lack of peace and happiness is often because we compare our lives and what we have with others. When we see what we are missing, we become unhappy, even if we were completely content before we knew about the difference. So, it is not what we have or do not have that makes us unhappy, but what other people have in comparison.

2. The other lesson is that the frustration and suffering of others negatively affects our emotional well being. Never wish for another human's suffering. If you hurt someone else, you will only be hurting yourself.

THE HAPPINESS GAME

Some people work hard, buy big houses and big cars, expensive jewellery and go on expensive vacations or take drugs to be happy. And yet, they easily become angry, sad and worry over petty things. They place a high value in the opinions and judgments of other people. They work hard and suffer for happiness; they travel thousands of miles to look for happiness and yet it is so fleeting in their lives. So, they need to get back to working hard in attempt to buy it again.

There are things that nature gave to all humanity equally, including the potential for happiness, love along with death and birth. You can add or take away nothing from these things. A man or woman who is happy, is just happy. A person in love, is a person in love. You cannot say my happiness or love is better than another person's love or happiness, because the things you love or make you happy are different, even though the feelings are the same. It is like eating an organic raw tomato from the same farm. No matter where you eat the tomato, whether it is in a mud hut or an expensive restaurant, the taste and nutrients you experience will be the same. Happiness, love, peace of mind and death are like that, they make us all equal.

If I am happy and loving, then I am as happy and loving as any man or woman on this earth - no worse, no better, but equally. I am as happy and loving as any human being who has ever lived, and as happy and loving as any human being who will ever live.

It is the same with death. The manner of death can vary greatly, but death is the same. In all cases, it is our soul that leaves our body. So, do not give away or give up on love, not for anyone and not for anything, no matter your status and no matter where you are living or your living conditions. You have as much capacity to find love as anyone else, it is your intrinsic right.

MAKING USE OF INNER INTELLIGENCE

The synchrony and infinitely complex way our body works tells us that the potential of infinite intelligence lies within us all. We are lucky and astronomically successful if we can even use only 10 percent of this infinite intelligence. Sometimes, you see the work of this infinite intelligence in the greatest human innovations and discoveries, such as flight, wireless communications, architecture, and art. Even all these discoveries and innovations are only a glimpse of this intelligence.

You must first know, accept, and believe that this intelligence does exist within you, as it did within any other of those men and women who made those great discoveries and innovations. You have the same potential, but you must work towards tapping into this infinite intelligence. Create a suitable environment and remove all doubts, veils and illusions that are creating your self-limitation. It is the greatest wealth, blessing, and beauty in this world. There is nothing impossible for this infinite intelligence within, and it has all of the answers to our questions. The knowledge of this power and its potential forms the components of your faith. Your doubts create your limitations.

Everyday, remove your doubts and reaffirm the presence and power of infinite intelligence. Only then will your power and intelligence grow. You will not need time and hard work for it to manifest. You will not see its work through what you receive externally, such as money or fame (although they are both potential manifestations). You will only see the power of this infinite intelligence through what you give, or what you do – in other words, in your ideas, inventions or discoveries. This infinite intelligence works through you, so you become the hollow pipe or medium of communication. The doubt, confusion, hardship, and limitations come when the egoistic mind thinks that it is the one doing the work, causing success or frustration. Remind yourself these eternal truths everyday and depend on the readiness of all knowing and infinitely powerful intelligence within.

Just like my thinking mind does not and cannot operate or control the workings of my digestive system, or the healing of my wounds, the thinking mind does not control or operate the work of infinite intelligence within. The mind becomes just a part of the suitable environment that allows the infinite intelligence within. The mind makes the conscious or subconscious choice and the infinite intelligence manifests through those choices. These are the invisible creations of the mind - the dominant or dwelling thoughts. The enlightened mind enables us to make the right choices consciously. The mind's responsibility is just to make the conscious or subconscious choices, but manifestation is the responsibility of the infinite intelligence within.

The failure and success of the mind is in what kind of choices it makes, not what happens after the choice or manifestation. The infinite intelligence can never fail to manifest the choices your thinking mind made. That is why we say, "God never fails."

GRATITUDE

Gratitude or living a grateful lifestyle is the most progressive life you can choose to live. Be eternally grateful for everything in your life. Be grateful for the visions, dreams, and faith you have, rather than wondering how you are going to achieve them. Follow your intuition and carry on with the small daily steps towards your goals. God will make it happen, not you. You do not have to see the whole staircase.

Being grateful for things before you receive them is a radical way of life because you say thank you for things you do not yet have physically. This is living a life of faith. Consider it received and thank as if you already have what you prayed for. Just know that it is not your hard work, analysis or other people that make your dreams come true, it is your faith and gratitude. If you say, "I have already received it," this is accepting and recognizing your prayers. Then, miracles will start happening. Faith and gratitude can move the mountains. You need no external validations or help from other people or their opinions. It is not your business to worry about how your goals will be accomplished, you need to simply say, "Thank you," and accept the vision you are given. The universe will begin to work in moving towards its accomplishment. Just saying thank you will change the vibration of the energy within you and turn it into positivity.

The greatest proof of your faith is gratitude. When you give thanks, you are expressing your faith, and by already accepting and receiving, you see what you prayed for as yours. Use the power of gratitude regularly. There is no grateful man or woman that is poor, sad, miserable, angry, or unhappy. A grateful heart is always cheerful, happy, content, calm, confident, healthy, abundant, and courageous.

PRAISE AND ALIGNMENT

All the power of infinite intelligence lies within you, but you can only use this power with the right alignment. You have the power to align the people and situations in your environment to either work for you or against you. The only way you make them work for you is through persistent and defiant gratitude. Gratitude is even more powerful than receiving the things you pray for because gratitude is based on faith. Your true power should be measured in terms of your gratitude.

There is some defiance and stubbornness that God encourages, and that is in faith. You cannot have two contradicting faith or beliefs. When you are grateful for something that you have still not received, you are aligning things in motion to work for you. In the face of your faith, everything is powerless to do anything contrary to that.

These principles also apply in case you have negative faith (ingratitude). No matter the abundance of resources in your environment, your negative faith will always lead you to poverty, misery, and other adversities in your life. Starve negativity by being grateful all the time. Just like a phantom-limb pain, the illusions of the past are giving you pain and misery in the present moment. Stop looking back - you are not going back there. Life is always forward.

7

Conscious And Subconscious Mind

CONSCIOUS LIVING

Conscious living is neither a careful nor a carefree life, it is a life of choice. Rather than seeing it as constantly being cautious or worrying about your thoughts and actions, see it as choosing to think, act and live in a certain way. Conscious living is not a lifestyle imposed on you, but rather it is choosing to live according to your free will. You are just exercising one of the greatest intrinsic rights and power with which God has endowed you.

THE CONSCIOUS AND SUBCONSCIOUS MIND

Is it possible for someone to make conscious poor choice? Is it possible to intentionally harm yourself? Even when a person commits suicide and the person intentionally, or consciously commits the act, the person lacks wisdom. You can be conscious, but ignorant. You can be intelligent, but unconscious. For you to make the right choices, you must be both wise and conscious.

THE CONSCIOUS MIND AND THE INFINITE INTELLIGENCE

The most important function of our conscious mind is the ability to choose negative or positive thoughts, choose how we react, what thoughts we have, our emotions and our actions. The conscious mind (the parliament or judiciary branch of our brain) makes the choice while the infinite intelligence within us (the executive branch) executes or implements the choices that we make. When the two become one, your conscious mind and infinite intelligence complement each other.

For example, when you choose to eat healthy food and have positive thoughts, the trillions of cells that sustain your life remain healthy. On the other hand, if you chose the unhealthy food (non-alignment or incongruity of the infinite intelligence and conscious mind), those cells become sick, weak, and eventually die. When they are weak and sick, you are weak and sick.

When your conscious mind works with infinite

intelligence within, then your life is full of joy, abundance, and good health. If you choose and do things in alignment with the infinite intelligence within, you can truly say "God is with me".

THE MIND

The mind can be a source of pain or joy, fear or courage, poverty, or wealth. I once watched an episode of the television show "Locked Up," where an inmate received a 76-year sentence after the attempted murder of another inmate. His original sentence had been less than five years for minor crimes, but his behaviour inside the prison kept him imprisoned for life. During his interview, he cried for his three children, wishing he could be with them. But the irony is that his actions and behavior at the prison contradicted his words. He regularly got into fights with other inmates, which sent him to isolation. His anger was not only affecting his life, but the lives of his loved ones. His mind had created a life of hell for him. He thought his actions would only hurt others, but in the end, they hurt him more. What are you enslaved by? Your mind can take you to hell or it can take you to heaven, so always be conscious that your thoughts and actions align.

If used as a good servant, the human mind can control

giant machines and rule over the physical world. It controls and creates complex financial models, discovers complex scientific theories and equations, invents great new technologies and transportation vehicles, imagines great philosophical ideas, makes great music and paintings. But humans are only able to achieve all these things, if the mind becomes a good servant. This can be achieved by living according to the natural laws and your personal principles and philosophies.

What sets apart the inventors, scientists, painters, musicians, and leaders from other people is their ability to direct their thoughts towards specific goals or purposes they set for themselves. Your ability to consciously guide your thoughts towards a worthy goal or purpose is what can set you apart.

CONQUERING THE MIND

In order to conquer the mind, you must learn how to live with and manage the little voice in your head. This does not mean silencing it, because each time you silence one thought, another one will come up - and there are thousands and thousands of them each day. Silencing your thoughts is like trying to chase after the wind or trying to fight your shadows.

Futile. The best way to deal with them is to observe and ignore these voices.

For example, if you have negative thoughts of worry or anxiety and you hear, "I am not good enough, I can't do this," observe the voice, and then ignore it. Focus on your faith, God or the infinite intelligence within. Only then will you have conquered your mind and become its master.

You would not tune in to a French radio channel and then hit the radio because it is not broadcasting in English. You would simply change the channel. That is how you should deal with the programming in your subconscious mind. Do not fight the subconscious mind, just change the programming within it. Change the channel or your original sins.

Just like anesthesia prevents your brain from processing pain during surgery, the mind can be controlled to deal with its thousands of demands, urges, and needs that can waste your life and energy. Even in solving other challenges in your life, look for the strategic point to control, rather than dealing with the thousands of manifestations of the damages or troubles created by ego.

HABITS OF THE MIND

There are many things that our brain has developed over years as habits which shape our lives, successes, and failures. But those habits are not who we are, we were just consciously or subconsciously programmed to have those habits. Sometimes your mind hates or dislikes to do something that is good for your life, such as waking up early, exercising or reading. These dislikes have nothing to do with who you are, your brain is simply not used to doing them, so it needs to be retrained. Make small changes to your routine every day that will make it easy for you to receive joy from those things you have been avoiding.

OWNERSHIP

People sometimes cling to their problems and develop a "victim identity." This is always evident when you try to tell a friend their problems are not a big deal or are illusions. They become angry because they feel a sense of identity loss. They subconsciously feel they are nobody without their deprived self-image, and disillusions. They have always lived as products of the reactions to their past experiences. They believe they are A because B happened to them.

Because these people are products of their

environment, they do not understand if you try to become something else. They expect you to live according to how the environment shaped you and what their impressions are of you. But to live freely according to your own will means living in freedom as a master.

THE ENVIRONMENT FOR TRILLION OF CELLS

Stress adversely affects our health by blocking our immune system and producing disease causing chemicals. This makes us vulnerable to infectious diseases, while the production of dangerous chemicals can lead to cancer, high blood pressure, diabetes, heart disease and more. Science has proven that our environment is primarily responsible for our health and that the environment acts as a culture where the cells grow. In your mind, that environment is made up of your perception and beliefs. If you have negative perceptions and beliefs that cause you stress, then you are providing a bad environment for your mind. The opposite of negative factors creates dopamine, oxycontin and other natural chemicals in the brain that make you happy and reduce stress. People often search for these natural chemicals in drugs or alcohol, to replicate the feeling of natural satisfaction.

THE TWO MENTALITIES

How you approach your life and the challenges within it affects not only the outcome, but also whether you are wasting your time and making the present moment unenjoyable.

I once read about a young woman named Kathie who had received a face transplant after she destroyed much of her face in a suicide attempt. After more than 20 painful surgeries on her face, she was left permanently disfigured. After the experience, she said her life was beautiful and she believed life was a gift to be cherished. Was this change in perspective due to her life being better than before her suicide attempt? Likely not. It was her perception that had changed. In her suicide attempt, she was trying to kill her old perception, not the body or the entity on the outside. If Kathie had had the same mentality or perception that she had when she attempted the suicide, we may not have ever heard those beautiful words from her.

It is not whether our situations are bad or good, it is our perception of those situations that determine not only our success, but also our desire to live.

PROTECT THE HEAD

I once watched a video of a fight between a monkey and a cobra. The monkey kept trying to bite the cobra's head from behind. The monkey knew if he got the head of the cobra, he could kill it, as the head is the most important and lethal part of its body. So, the cobra kept ducking and swinging to prevent a head bite. Animals often protect the most vulnerable parts of their bodies in different ways.

For humans, the head is also the most important and powerful part of human body, and the most vulnerable. The head is the source of your peace of mind, your creativity, your perceptions, and self-image and so on. When people try to finish you off by attacking your head or the source, how ignorant is it to leave it unprotected? You could be letting others inside your head to give you worry, fear, negative self-image, and hate. Do not surrender your head, you must protect it like the cobra. You also allow others into your head if you are jealous of their success, or if you don't wish them well or if you have negative thoughts about them. This philosophy is part of the natural laws you must follow to have a happy life.

8

Self-Image

THE SKIN AS AN ORGAN

The skin is the largest human organ. Our bodies are just entities composed of sextillion microorganisms that form organs adapted for different functions. Most of our problems come from our strong attachment and identification with our cover, our skin or facial appearance, which is just one of the organs that makes up our bodies. We discriminate ourselves or others based on the appearance or the color of this organ. We even drive our self-worth and values system based on it, even though the appearances and colors of all the other organs are the same.

The identification with our skin and its appearance is so deeply ingrained that we sometimes do harmful things to our other organs. This egoistic identification with our facial appearance and the names given to us lead us to hate and discriminate other people. Those feelings are then harmful to our other organs, but we overlook the harm because we are ignorantly focused on the "me," which is our face and name. When scientists make medicines, they do not say for this face, skin color or name. They make medicines for humans – for the organs and systems within us, to bring them back to health. Natural laws are also the same. They work for everyone and they do not discriminate between faces, names, or skin colours.

Sometimes, when a doctor tells a patient not to eat certain foods, such as fast food or sweets, the patient does not understand. The advice conflicts with their experience of what is good food. They experience cognitive dissonance and find it difficult to adopt to the new healthy diet. It is the same when a patient is asked to face his fears or trauma through prolonged exposure for healing, or when someone is asked to forgive his abusers or people who hurt him. The egoistic identity of "me" - the face and name - could not understand the values of forgiveness, love, and peace of mind. It does not understand how these things are good not only for all the other organs, but also for the "me." Just like medicine, positive thoughts and feelings are good for all organs, and for all human beings. They are universal.

THE MENTAL CEILING

A mental ceiling is when you have set a ceiling for yourself based on your past self-image, or from the by-product of your past invisible creations or programming. These ceilings are created subconsciously, and they prevent you from reaching any higher in your career, creativity, happiness, or abundance. When you live under this ceiling, your progress in life is severely limited or handicapped.

Here you can see the bubbles you may be trapped in or under. When you are under the ceiling, your upward movement is limited. Therefore, you are restricted to horizontal movement. Many people change their jobs, their location, buy expensive things – all with the hope of feeling better and moving up. It is like a sick man changing from a wooden to a golden bed, hoping for relief. The same miserable person with deprived self-image and other negative thoughts will be moving horizontally from one job to another, from one city to another, from one marriage to another, but the bubble in which he is trapped is the same.

The movements only provide a temporary sense of relief and happiness.

For true change to take place, and to be healed from the negative experience in which you are trapped, you must break through the ceiling. When you live above the ceiling, the sky is the limit for you. You use the past negative self-image and failure as a steppingstone to launch you upwards.

Sometimes people who have broken through the bubble end up moving back under it. That is, going back to live in the past. The individual falls back, or regresses, into the habits of deprived or negative self-image, faulty programming, disillusions, ignorance, and other by-products of your past invisible creations.

The ceiling is made of other people's negative opinions of you, as well as your own negative sense of self-image born from failures and past experiences. Also preventing you from moving up is the culture, religion, and conventions in which you were born, along with the societal expectations and standards of your success and value systems.

The only way you can break through the mental ceiling is by faith. You should completely renounce your past deprived self-image, negative thoughts, and attitudes you previously accepted and focus only on your invisible creations or faith in the present moment.

TRUST YOURSELF

Doubt has never achieved anything but failure in all human history. In your life, you have no other option but to trust yourself and your own intuition. When facing a decision, you will always be presented with several choices. Remember, you are the best judge and decision maker for your life. Do not value anybody's opinion more than your own. Nobody else is living your life; sharing your feelings of hurt, happiness, stress, or frustration. Nobody else can truly understand your feelings.

THE SALTY OPINION

How you see yourself is one of the most important powerful resources you have to change the world. That self-image is what I call your saltiness. At the beginning of your career, before you achieved any success, people did not recognize you as anything or anyone important. It is as if you were a stone. This can sometimes kill your dreams or, your saltiness, if you accept their opinions of you.

Mostly people do not understand what you are doing, and they only believe in the conventional visible world and its order of values. They only believe in limitations and scarcity. You must forgive their ignorance and ignore their opinions. They are projecting their own fears and limitations upon you, unaware of the true reality and infinite power and intelligence that lies within each man and woman.

Poise comes from knowing that you are the only one who can accept or recognize your saltiness. You are not made or created by someone else, nor are you defined by their external validation or recognition. Your equanimity comes from this true independence. This wisdom about the source of your confidence, gives you an unshakable foundation from which you can draw creativity, enthusiasm, and drive to achieve goals larger than your life. Those who feel their gifts or talents were given to them by someone else live in fear of losing them and exist in a state of mental slavery because they fear talents can be taken from them.

This wisdom of saltiness teaches us two things. First, if you fail to love and bless yourself, fail to see the infinite intelligence and infinite abundance of God within you, you live your life in self-doubt and negative self-image. In this case, you are the salt that lost its saltiness, so you have no use for the world, and you will be cast out. Second, this wisdom teaches us how one can be made salty again. This is something only you can do for yourself. Develop a positive self-image, courage, self-confidence, thoughts of abundance and gratitude. Again, no man can take these from you either, it is out of their control and influence.

Whenever you try to portray yourself as one person in public, but you are another in private, this contravenes the natural laws and you will face consequences. This is because you are living in chaos. You cannot be salt in public and sand in private. Imagine trying to live in righteousness and depravity at the same time, or with the devil and God simultaneously. It is better to end the suffering and choose to be with God.

Next time you ask yourself why you failed, you should answer, "It was because I didn't love myself enough." If you are not gracious enough to bless yourself with a positive self-image, then no one can. No amount of money or material wealth, or professional skills or certificates will give you your saltiness. It all comes from within. Love yourself unconditionally, have a positive self-worth and a righteous life and self-image. At one time, when Donald Trump was $8 billion in debt, he pointed to a homeless man and said to his daughter Ivanka, "That man is $8 billion richer than me." He was referring to material wealth, but the self-image Trump had was still much more than the homeless man, and so Trump went on to be successful, nevertheless. Self-image is the only thing that matters, not the material wealth. A stone cannot pass itself as a ruby or a diamond. Be the ruby or the diamond and the world will value you likewise.

BE THE LIGHT FIRST

A bulb that is not turned on cannot give you light, just as you cannot see the bulb as it is in darkness. If you are in darkness yourself, how do you expect others to see you, or to give off light? Be the light first and then others cannot avoid your brightness. They will be drawn to you. If a man stands in darkness and asks others to come and share his light, they will see that as the talk of a madman. Love yourself and your life first, in order to love others. Heal yourself first to heal others. Be strong first to give strength to others. Be confident and courageous first to give confidence and courage to others. Be faithful first to teach others faith. Be the light first, to give others light.

The world or other people only want to see the fruit, not the hard work that goes into producing it. They only appreciate the fruits. But the farmers know that there would be no fruit without the planting, watering, and taking care of the plant. Do not let anyone cut down the plant or destroy the seedling because they do not yet see fruit. And do not let them destroy your dreams. As long as you know in your heart that you are doing something worthwhile, and you love doing it, then never stop. The monetary reward will come later.

PICTURE OF VULNERABILITY

If you see yourself as vulnerable, then others will see you that way, too. Even though you see yourself as vulnerable of other people's decisions, authorities, and the economic environment, you are simply the manifestation of your thoughts.

If you feel you are vulnerable to death, sickness, failing, not finding a job, losing a job, and not having enough success, you are really saying, "I am not good enough," or, "I don't have enough." And if you worry that you do not have enough, then you will not – until you change your thoughts and perceptions.

In those moments, you need courage, confidence, and fearlessness. It is believing that you do have enough of everything that you felt vulnerable about.

Feeling of vulnerability is enslavement by the egoistic mind. It is what keeps you poor and scarce and it steals away your happiness. It is the fountain of misery that wastes your life.

IDENTIFYING WITH ILLUSIONS

Do not say I have mental illness, instead say, "I have temporary or passing illusions." These illusions can be negative self-esteem, fear, self-doubt, anxiety, worry, hate, guilt or regret. Some of the illusions we have are long held beliefs from years of recurring thoughts. These thoughts can last only a short time, but they still need to be dealt with by simply observing and ignoring them.

Some thoughts or illusions have been with you for years, on the other hand. These are created by incorrect perceptions and opinions about who you are. So, how can you overcome them? Despite their seeming permanence, you can use the same method. Observe and ignore the thoughts. In this case, however, you replace those thoughts with a consciously created self-image or identity. You consciously choose who you want to be, then assume those roles immediately. There is absolutely nothing wrong with the assumption of roles in this life for practical purposes, just like actors are assigned roles in a movie. The height, length or location of a wave does not mean it is a separate entity from the ocean. The waves come in different shapes, heights and lengths and crash at different time. They are all temporary. It is the same with our roles in this world, they come at different times, with different purposes and positions.

But you only live once as that wave. So, choose your role carefully and play it seriously in this short and precious life we have. Your roles should be consciously created and guided by wisdom to create a good life for you and others. Your role will be the contribution you make to this world. Remember, you did not come to this world to take, you came here to give.

TYRANNY OF THE FALSE SELF

The tyranny of the false self is largely underestimated and not well-recognized by many. The ignorance of who we really are, and the existence of the egoistic identity has blinded us from seeing our true and potential selves. What is holding you back? The simple answer, it is the ego.

For most people, the tyrant of false self is the greatest thief of vital energy, time, happiness, and creativity. The tyrant only cares about compliments and opinions, status and accomplishments, fame, and money. The ego has a limited understanding of itself and the world around it as it has entirely identified itself with the old programming. Even a slight perceived injury or attack to it becomes a major issue for "self," such that it begins attacking itself through self-loathing. You become like a dog chasing its tail in a circle. You are full of defense and fighting strategy for the endless war or conflicts with yourself.

Focus on what you do and not your ego, other people's opinions, or their compliments. You are here as a representative of light energy and you are the manifestation of that. Your ray is so unique and different that no other human being was born like you. All you have is this time, this moment, before you transform to another form or vehicle, but the same light energy will occupy that vehicle. This is how the light energy keeps transforming, never dying, with no beginning and no end. It is the eternal continuous transformation from one form to another, through life and through death. With this knowledge, you do not need to be afraid of negative opinion or shame. No one and nothing can get a hold of your soul, spirit, the light energy, or fields. This part of you is untouchable and deathless. Your old programming and egoistic identities prevented you from seeing your true self. You must awaken the light in you.

CHANGING FORTUNES

The wise use challenging times to grow stronger, confident, and wiser while the ignorant are broken and weakened by them. It is only those times of defeat, failure, poverty, and humiliation that create the perfect environment for the growth of your fortitude. If you are broken down and weakened by those challenging conditions and become fearful or humiliated, then the challenging situations have defeated you. Nothing can compare to the infinite intelligence within you. When you learn to value what you have within, then you can create value in your life (become the salt and light of the world). The level to which you value the infinite intelligence within you determines the level of your success in life. If you believe the infinite intelligence within you has no value, then you will never have value. How do you create this value? By being grateful for all the blessings in your life and considering as received whatever you prayed for.

Every new day gives you an opportunity to have a fresh start or live in a new mindset, to either live in faith or hang on to your past illusions. Do not see yourself as a worm and blame the world for seeing you as such. It is what you give out that the world sees or receives, so give out light, hope, love, and courage.

NEGATIVE IMAGINATIONS

When you start to respond to imaginary attacks, arguments, and reactions from other people, this is a form of self-attack that fools you into thinking that you are attacking your imaginary enemy. Such people become weak, powerless, and vulnerable when the real attack comes, because they have spent so much mental energy and focus on the imaginary attack. When the real threat comes, they find they have exhausted their energy and time fighting illusions. Stop wasting your energy and time on imaginary enemies, arguments, responses or trying to justify your opinions in your head.

The other dangers and disadvantages of fighting, arguing, and responding to imaginary enemies or attackers is that your visualization and mental dwelling on these attacks can make them your reality, since they are your invisible creations. Thinking in terms of getting attacked by other people means you see yourself as a victim of other people's attacks. This makes you feel vulnerable and is a negative self-image that usurps your power, strength, love, health, abundance, and happiness. Treat those thoughts as wandering away of the mind and focus on making real changes in your life.

Getting into imaginary fights or responding to attacks also lower your standard. The energy it takes to visualize the attack and retaliation wastes your time and energy, just as real fights and attacks do.

You must limit all the detraction and the times you do not feel like working and remind yourself that these moments separate the great from the average. The great will not allow the feelings of laziness or other people stop them from doing their job.

Every day, we face challenges that either waste our time or build us up. Choose activities that will improve your life, such as working on your dreams, improving your health by eating healthy and working out and learning new skills that can improve your earning power, emotional intelligence and spirituality.

SELF-MENTAL ABUSE

The main source of mental abuse often comes from yourself, even if you feel others mentally abuse you as well. Mental abuse comes from your fear, your concerns about what others think of you, hate, anger, ingratitude, self-loathing, and regret. There is nothing to achieve by carrying around such a heavy burden. Success cannot come to you when you are living in a state of mental abuse. Free yourself first.

SELF-PRESERVATION

Self-preservation is the only consistent and enduring characteristic of all living things. Animals in the wild either hunt for food or die of hunger. If humans reached a level of food scarcity, humans would likely kill each other to survive as well. Not only has it become the survival of the physically fittest, but also the survival of the mentally fittest and emotionally fittest, which means great abundance, wealth, and happiness for the most wise or intelligent.

You must have a positive self image to thrive, and you must have great courage, wisdom, peace of mind, happiness, and good health. When you have these, then you are preserving yourself.

The principle of self-preservation is a universal self-evident truth. At the centre, there is self. That is why I have said do not lose yourself or your saltiness or you will be thrown out and trampled on the ground. We learn self-preservation from animals – from the beautiful birds in the air to the lions on the land to the majestic sharks and whales in the sea - they are all involved in the activities of self-preservation every day. The whole universe has adapted over time to ensure its survival, through adaptations to the environment, to survival tactics and hunting techniques. Self-preservation is one of the greatest lessons we can learn from nature. The more you value yourself, the more you thrive.

Life rewards the brave because the infinite intelligence within can only be expressed by courage. God is jealous when you put anyone or anything before him or her - money, power, careers, another man or woman, love, peace, talents, or skills. This is the same as idle worshipping or putting something or someone else before God. The infinite intelligence requires this same supreme confidence and courage to communicate. Become the hollow pipe and remove all doubts and fears.

9

Choosing God

CONFIDENCE IN GOD

A great majority of the world's population believe in God or some form of deity. Their faith and beliefs enable them to witness miracles, receive healings and achieve great success in their lives or careers. The power of believing or faith is undeniable. Sometimes people with less formal education have achieved greater things in life than people who are educated, perhaps because they have greater faith or confidence in God than educated people who perhaps analyze everything and every move in their lives. Believe in something, no matter how the external reality looks or what others think of it. Be a misfit proudly. I believe, almost everything in this world can be achieved through faith, not through the analytical mind. The analytical mind is a servant of faith and the subconscious mind. You must actively ignore the self-limiting ideas of the conscious mind (the servant) and always remain strong in your faith. We all have this infinitely powerful tool (faith) to achieve anything in our lives. Believe in the process. It has never failed over the thousands of years human beings have been on this earth.

Children naturally turn all their learnings into faith. Their subconscious minds wholly accept all the information they learn in their early years, because they do not have a filter system. It is the conscious, or analytical, mind that creates doubt through its filtering system based on societal programming or conventional wisdom and the past. With the analytical mind as the master of your subconscious mind, you compare, contrast, and analyze new wisdoms or natural laws that go against conventional wisdom or programming. This fills your mind with doubts and skepticism, as you try to reconcile your old and new experiences into their new boundaries. Therefore, what you can do and what you can be is limited. To be free from doubts, you must break free from this mental prison.

BELIEVE IN YOUR GOD

It does not matter what religion you follow, or what type of God you believe in. The important thing is that you believe. There are many different religions and beliefs in the world, and the followers receive miracles and blessings from their Gods everyday.

The followers who have doubt, weak beliefs or are not serious with their faith, receive almost nothing.

Many people hate and fear the devil, but still do the devil's work by living their lives with hate, vengeance, unforgiveness, jealousy and abuse. Do not honor or value what is not Godly.

And many separate from their God for petty reasons. If you run, you will bare the weight of your burdens and break, suffering from the hardships. If you stay with God, your challenges will feel light, and you will gain wisdom and strength. Your circumstances will change to bless you more, your decision- making will improve from this position of power, love, peace of mind and abundance. You will unleash the infinite power of God. Everything in your world, body and soul will have a different vibration and energy – the positive energy of God.

Material poverty is a disease that makes some people sick, but makes the righteous wise, as the bond with God grows stronger. But for the wicked, material scarcity separates them from God, and they live in misery with other misfortunes. It is the same with wealth. Material gains make the wicked ignorant, greedy, unhappy, and heartless, but makes the righteous generous, happy, and more loving.

The other means to live with God is to love yourself and your life. Did you ever try to spend a day with someone you do not like? Maybe you stayed in the same house, or worked in the same office? The days seem endless, the hours move slowly, with a tension and negativity that increases, while draining your energy and blocking your creativity. Imagine if the person you disliked was you. You would have to spend everyday in that environment, with the tension and anxiety rising all the time. Do you see the damage you can do to yourself? Never deny yourself love.

Do not be jealous of those living a life of abundance or courage. They have chosen to live with God, and you are equipped to make the same choice. Just as you are equipped to make choices that make your life miserable and poor. Choose to live with God and all good things will be yours.

Make the best of the life you were given - it is a gift.

IT IS NEVER A LOSS

No transaction or expectation should ever separate you from God. If you separate from God while searching for success, money, or good health you will become fearful, worried, and anxious and not find what you were looking for. You sought wealth to feel abundant and secure. You sought success to feel good. When you are with God, you achieve those feelings, so why separate from Him in pursuit of them in the first place? No amount of money or success can replace God or make you feel complete, fulfilled, or contented, without also having His presence in your life. God never said, "Make a lot of money or achieve success to be worthy of me, or to have my presence in your life." These are all illusions that lead to discontentment and a sense of unfulfillment. Nothing you achieve externally can fill the void left by God's absence in your life. If I cannot find God in this now, I will never find him anywhere else, or at any other time.

As I stated in my first book, seeking God in the future is one of the greatest sins you can commit. It is the devil's trick that says, "wait for tomorrow." The successes or achievements you thought you lost because you chose to stay with God rather than sell your soul to the devil are not lost. You will reap the fruit of choosing to stay with God. God will abundantly bless you and you will move on to better things. Your faith in God will be handsomely rewarded. While you wait, doubt not. Your loyalty to God and your faith will surely reward you with abundant blessings. You will only lose if you chose the devil or sold your soul. In all the interactions in human history, no man or woman has ever lost for choosing to stay with God.

You will know you have won the game by choosing to stay with God because your inner intuition will tell you. You do not have to wait for the physical or external manifestation, simply listen to yourself. Your decisions to stay with God will manifest internally, in the form of serenity, courage, joy and peace of mind. These will in turn create the foundation for your success externally, or in the material world.

You need God most when you start having self-attacking or self-limiting thoughts and when you start hating or despising your life. That is exactly when you should reaffirm firmly your choice to stay with God. Do not be fooled into thinking of staying with God only when your life is at its best. Your choice to stay with God should be in good and bad times as well, for better or worse. These challenging times are the best reminders of affirming your choice to stay with God.

YOU CANNOT BYPASS GOD

When you are typing on a computer, you type your message and it can be printed out onto a piece of paper. It is the same with your mind. You (your conscious mind) type your message on your PC (God, Allah, Jesus or others – these are the brands), and the printout is your reality. So, nothing happens without you, and nothing happens without God. In other words, the paper will not print out (the reality will not manifest), without you or the PC. You cannot bypass God, and God cannot bypass you with regards to what is happening in your life.

MELODRAMA OF THE EGO

Give a man or a woman 1,000 years to deal with the melodrama of the ego and it will not be enough for him or her. You should not fight the ego or try to change the ego because no amount of time will suffice to win. You cannot perfect the ego by jumping from one identity (self-image) of the ego to another. The best way to deal with ego is to ignore it. A life lived with ego is a life of illusions and lies. But it is you who accepted those negative gifts because you chose to separate from the infinite intelligence within.

These illusions are also created when you create excuses for your unhappy life. You believe it is because you lack a good education, for example, or because you did not have good parents or good connections for work. If you believe you do not have it, then you will never have it. There are many who do not have these things and face hardships from a life of abuse, but still go on to succeed and change the world. Despite the adversity in their lives, they chose to stay with God and were made stronger.

YOU ARE ON YOUR OWN

If you consciously or subconsciously decide to become hateful, vengeful or unforgiving, God will not be on your side because you will have covered God with layers and layers of dirt. God is not in those things; you can only find God in their opposites. This is not based on evidence from one life, or even thousands of lives, it is based on billions of lives over many generations. This is a self-evident truth.

Avoid thoughts of weakness hurt, victimhood or blame. Even if they happened to you, renounce them. Do not speak of them. Focus instead on your strength, power, opportunity, talents, gifts, and the good things that have happened to you. If you dwell on negativity, then you have accepted it as a gift. Only accept the good gifts, such as grace and friendship.

What is rationality any way? It is rationalizing or justifying ideas or theories based on your past knowledge. If your past knowledge is incorrect or is based on illusions, then your rationale is based on ignorance. That is what happens when you rationalize your self-limiting thoughts and scarcities based on your past identities, created by ignorance.

THE MOST IMPORTANT CHOICE

Isn't it interesting that despite the way billions of people die, the soul is taken away just the same? Whether it is a brutal or cruel death, or a peaceful or merciful death, death is just a transition from one world to another. Death is like birth in this way. It does not matter where or how you were born; it is still just a birth – an entity coming or transitioning into this world from your mother's womb. Birth and death make us equal, but what happens in between is what we make of our lives. In between, one of the most important choice you make in your life is to choose to have faith in God.

Regardless of what life brings you, God will always make a way for you. The alternative is a life of misery and pain. You may feel you have the most legitimate and convincing excuses why you chose not have faith in God, but in the end, it is your life and your choice.

BLASPHEMY OF THE HOLY SPIRIT

To sin is to be ignorant in thoughts, words, and actions. When you violate the natural laws, you will suffer in life, that is the cost of sin. The sickness of the spirit happens when your conscious mind works out of sync with the current of life or the natural laws. When your cells do not function normally, you get physical ailments, and when you go against natural laws, your spirit gets sick. The external manifestations of this sickness include fear, doubt, and other negative thoughts and feelings. The long years of illusions have separated you from your natural state, making it difficult to go back because you are so used to living in abnormality.

When you have positive and healthy thoughts, then you are in your natural state and functioning normally spiritually. People with thoughts of abundance, confidence and serenity are functioning according to the infinite intelligence within.

The endless pit of a spiritual black hole that swallows infinite human lives is made of ignorance. I believe the greatest evil on Earth is ignorance, followed by judgement. The fixation of measuring the ignorance of other people is just another form of ignorance. Two wrongs cannot make one right. What you are measuring with judgment is changing you at the same time, because you are pulled into the vortex of the spiritual black hole. Soon, you will find yourself in an endless cycle of measuring and judging other people, while ignoring your own faults. This critical and judgemental attitude will blind you from seeing any positives in the other person and will consume you. Do not be pulled into the darkness of judgment, or the weakness or sins of other people. You will be pulled into the darkness with them. Stay in light, be the light and shine for others.

Each time you count the scarcities or blessings of another, you pocket one for yourself. Whatever sins or weaknesses of others you are measuring, you are also being immersed in the same sin or weakness. You cannot smear others with dirt, without getting your hands dirty.

THE OCEAN AND THE WAVE

You are just a wave among the gazillions of waves, along with every other plant or living thing in the universe. Each wave has a unique energy and has a unique contribution. The ocean is God (the infinite intelligence). The ocean can survive without the waves, but the waves cannot survive without the ocean. When the wave hits the shore (death), it becomes part of the ocean again as the water retreats, but only to become another wave again. This cycle of birth, death and rebirth continues eternally, as energy can neither be created nor destroyed. According to the natural laws of energy conservation, energy can only be converted from one form of energy to another.

We are all part of this ocean, and hence, a part of God. A wave cannot say, "I am the ocean." But his or her intelligence is that of God's, and their strength and power come from the ocean. The intelligence of God is deep, just like the depth of the ocean compared to the depth of a single wave.

SPIRITUAL DESENTIZERS

When you get a nerve injury on your hands, the physiotherapists may give you desensitizers that help prevent your nerves from sending pain messages to your brain. With regular exercise, you slowly get used to touching and rubbing your hands together again, as your nerves become less sensitive. We need such desensitizers spiritually; these are the small challenges and discomforts we face daily. These desensitizers enable your conscious mind to accept and overcome challenges without becoming anxious, nervous, and fearful.

No matter your level of success or satisfaction in life, challenges will still come your way everyday. You will lose loved ones, you will lose money, you will face criticism and have health scares or become sick. There are many challenges to face in life. Do not try to avoid them, think instead about how you can respond to them. Use those situations to grow spiritually and intellectually.

CELEBRATING SUCCESS

In order to make the world a better place by helping the poor or giving your time and energy in service to other people, you must first learn to celebrate the successes of another person. If you celebrate another person's success, the success is also yours. There is no success or achievement in this world that is not yours and your successes also belong to the world. There is something to cheer about everyday. Showing love, gratitude, forgiveness and celebrating the success of others will expand your world.

In the past, you were empty because you told God and the universe, "If you do not give me blessings or abundance, then I will recognize no abundance or blessings in this world." So, you remained in scarcity. This is a giving world. So, even those who have everything will eventually leave it for the world. Even what the Pharaohs thought had taken to their graves for the next life, are now museum exhibition.

10

The How And Attitude

MR. BUSYBODY

With so much time spent on complaining, is it any wonder there is no time left for your own endeavours? When you use your energy to focus on other people rather than focus on your work, you are hurting your own chances of success. By coveting the achievements and wealth of others, you lose that time to work on your projects. When you claim victimhood, you lose the opportunity to create a happy, joyful life. If you are only allowing yourself to spend a quarter of your energy on improving your own life, how can you wonder why you are failing? Even a small reduction in worrying about others will improve your chances of success in your own goals. Take some time to write down what thoughts and obsessions are wasting your energy and time. Then, deal with them and move on. You will see how you were the one making things difficult for yourself.

Instead of watering and taking care of The Crops, you were taking care of The Weeds.

It was Isaac Newton who discovered the laws of gravity from observing a falling apple. Prior to that, many people had also witnessed a falling apple, but it was Newton who made discovery of gravity. Why? This is because Newton was not distracted by petty thoughts and was consciously focused on his study of the natural laws. Simple observation and intuition gave him the answer, or the truth that had always been in the universe.

This is the same for Archimedes, who jumped out of swimming pool shouting "Eureka!" So many others before him had jumped into pools, but it was Archimedes who discovered how to measure the volume of a liquid through the displacement of a mass immersed in it. This is because he was observant and focused on science all the time.

If you have been feeding your energy and time to the hyenas, they will never say thank you. They will never help or improve your life in anyway. You are the one choosing to feed them, so take responsibility for this choice. It is impossible to undo the past, so focus on your present moment and your work. Analyzing and trying to undo or correct the past will only further waste your time and energy. Not even

God will undo what happened yesterday, so focus on what is important in your life right now with positive thoughts, actions and energy.

STOP LOOKING FOR PERFECTION

Stop setting conditions for your success and looking for perfection in your personal growth in order to feel worthy. Many have wasted time doing this and held back God's grace and blessings in the process. Also, remember that other people's measures of success, perfection and excellence do not apply to you. Who are the people who set those standards? Who are they to you? What business do they have in what you do? Where were they during your struggles?

The spiritually immature person recruits a master for himself because he has adapted to being subordinate - being told what to do, and how to do it. So, even when he is working alone, he values the opinions of other people. He wonders if he has met the standards and measures of success set by society and looks for approval and validation. Nobody has the monopoly over truth, philosophy, wisdom, creativity, or talent. Shine as you are, in whatever gifts God has blessed you with.

THE ILLUSION OF FREE TIME

Rather than filling your time listening to the news, checking social media, or playing video games all the time, take time everyday to listen to yourself. Recently, I stopped playing music in my car so that I could simply drive in silence so I could hear myself. It is a very exciting experience. It is better to have negative thoughts you can hear than have your thoughts covered up by other activities.

Ignorance is the source of negative thoughts, so if you are wise, you can receive lessons or enlightenment. My wisdom has come from my ignorance. I have transmuted my negative thoughts into knowledge. When you fill your time with trivial pursuits such as video games and social media, you deny yourself the opportunities of transmutation and enlightenment. You limit the time you have for spiritual listening. Therefore, there is no growth. Everything you do in this life comes at a cost of not doing something else. There is no free time in this life, there is either wasted time or a time used well.

REJECTION AND FAILURE

I once witnessed an eagle kill a baby warthog in the African wilderness. The warthog was struggling to free himself from the grips of the eagle's sharp claws. This is common. Prey tries to get away from its predator in a struggle of life and death for both. The relationship between predator and prey highlights the rejections and failures in life. Some people are paralyzed by the fear of rejection and failure because they have been rejected or have failed in life. Imagine a lion giving up his practice of hunting because he was unsuccessful one time. The prey will not come to the lion and offer himself up as a meal? Just like success will not simply appear in your life for the taking. Rejection and failures are more common than success. I heard once that for every 10 cancer treatment experiments, nine are failures. This means billions of dollars are spent on failed experiments and trials, along with countless hours of research and study. But, the research continues, despite the knowledge that it is statistically likely to fail. Even though the odds are against them, they continue. If you have failed nine times in your life, will you be back and try for the 10th time? One or two attempts does not equal failure. Life is in the struggle. It is not a destination, so dust up and go for it again.

SELF-DEFEAT AND SELF-CONFIDENCE

If you have no self-confidence, you have defeated yourself before your enemy has even touched you. All the enemy has to do is walk over you and move on, because you are already a dead man. Your spirit is in the casket waiting to rejoin with your body at death. When you do not live by your principles and value yourself – when you lose your saltiness - you become a fearful, scarce, and poor person. How can you beat up yourself like that? Remain true to your principles – you live and die by them.

If you indulge in negative self-talk, saying, "I am not good at this," you are self-inflicting defeat. It is as if you are on the soccer pitch and you keep scoring against your own team. How can you expect to win such a game? Start playing for your team if you expect to win anything. If you are helping your opponents defeat you, they will win. Nobody will play for you, so play for yourself. Nobody will leverage them for you. There is a famous butcher from Turkey nicknamed Salt Bae who has opened great steakhouses around the world that are now frequented by celebrities and athletes. If a simple butcher can leverage his skills like that, and achieve wealth and notoriety, what about the skills you have?

ON THE VALUE OF TIME

Imagine if Steve Jobs allowed his engineers to relax and finish their projects at whatever pace they wanted. This would allow for procrastination and laziness, and who knows what innovations would still be left unrealized? Distraction and complacency would have seeped in, perhaps key talents would have left the company, and Steve Jobs would not have become the innovator of the personal computers and devices so many have today. Steve Jobs knew the value of time and the dangers of procrastination and laziness (some of the greatest wasters of talents). Imagine the other great talents that have died in history before realizing their true potential. They wasted the gift of the infinite intelligence within them before being allowed to sing the songs in their hearts. These accomplishments have been left unfounded not because people did not wish to achieve something great in their lives, it is because they believed they would always have tomorrow to complete them. They did not have a sense of urgency or a real understanding of the value of time. To achieve success, time must be included as a major component in the formula.

Success of a Project = Time + Talent

Without time, success or talent cannot exist. Your talents are useless if you have no time to use them, your success will not be possible. When the first Macintosh computers came out, they dazzled the world. But now, they are seen as obsolete technologies, because time has passed. If you are not careful, your great idea or project will also become obsolete before you have the chance to show it to the world.

I value my project because it is important now, not at any other time or in the future. The greatest world discoveries, innovations or new ideas are all useless if they came out at the wrong time.

WHAT YOU BREAK IS THE PERCEPTION

There is something called a reality distortion zone, where innovators are pushed to produce beyond their seeming capabilities or what was thought of as possible. Henry Ford and Steve Jobs both encouraged their engineers to break through their old perceptions of what was impossible. I believe the phenomenon should be called the perception distortion zone, not the reality distortion zone.

DO NOT TRY TO BECOME EVERYTHING

Have you ever been looking for work and found yourself applying for every position that has become available? If you try to be everything to everyone, you are allowing someone else to decide who you become. Then, you may spend the rest of your life in that position, even though it was not a decision made by you. Find what you really love doing and follow your passion with all of your heart and energy. The people who know their purpose in life know where to focus their time and energy. A mango tree only produces mangos, just as an apple tree only produces apples. They cannot become other fruits, just because someone else wants them to. Decide what tree you want to be and serve well in that position. Give it all you have, with every fiber in your body, and let the universe say, "Here stood a really good mango tree (philosopher, nurse, teacher, accountant, poet, musician, or footballer). Take pride in what you love to do.

Trying to do everything in life shows a lack of focus. When you disperse your life energy in so many directions, these waves of energy are too weak to achieve anything meaningful. You cannot send all your armies in different directions if you want to win a war - you must place them in only a few strategic positions.

SICKENING YOURSELF FOR WORK

I have seen some people chew tobacco or drink energy drinks daily to keep themselves alert and energized at work. These habits are unhealthy and could ultimately lead to unwanted medical conditions. In an effort to be productive, they will face consequences that will affect their lives in negative ways – far beyond their current employment. Taking drugs to stay alert will eventually create a health issues that could incapacitate you and reduce your productivity. The day you understand your self-worth, your life will change.

When you sell your soul for a piece of the world, you are betraying the more than 60 trillion soldiers (cells) who are highly trained and working for you. They will never be able to build or create any kingdom on this earth.

There is an expression "Work smarter, not harder." Working smart means choosing the right career and industry that is growing and scalable - a career that needs your brain, rather than your muscle and time for growth. It is something you love, that does not belittle you or rob you of dignity or personal health.

FOR THE LOVE OF THE GAME

If you want to be great in something you do, look to the people who have already achieved success in those fields, and observe how they perceive what they are doing. You will find that many of them enjoy what they are doing. Few people start a new project with clenched teeth, focused only on making money. If there is no natural interest, the endeavour will fail, no matter how hard they work, because it was a failure from the beginning. They started the career to earn a living, not for the love of the game.

If it is not enjoyable, then you are torturing yourself. This is like marrying just to have children, rather than marrying for love and to enjoy life together. Having children is good, just like earning a living. But at what cost? Why not also marry someone you love, or work in a career you enjoy? Who is preventing you from doing that? Only yourself. These achievements are not reserved for a few special people. You have the choice to have these successes in your life.

It is never too late for love, no matter how old you are. When you find love, it changes your whole life or existence. You become more alive, experience boundless energy and excitement. Each minute of your life becomes more enjoyable. It is better to experience hardship doing what you love, rather than doing what you don't love with ease. It is like doing chores in a loveless marriage - difficult and frustrating. But doing chores when you are in a loving relationship (or when you are living a happy life alone), is easy and enjoyable. If you fear following your heart because you think it is too late or you are afraid of the challenge, then try doing something you don't love and experience the mental torture and boredom of getting through each day.

WHAT DO YOU DO WITH COURAGE AND FAITH?

What do you do with the courage, fearlessness, contentment, and faith you acquire in your life? If you do not use them, you will go to your grave with them. I do not want to be the most courageous or fearless person in the graveyard. Having these traits means nothing if you are not using them – they may even atrophy if you do not use them. How can you use these traits to improve your life, or help you achieve your dreams? What if you die tonight or tomorrow? Will you have used your courage, fearlessness, and faith? How will you rate yourself on how much you have utilized each of those virtues?

Your thinking mind should consciously plan and strategize on how to use these traits in your everyday life practically. Then, write down the challenges in using them, so you can learn.

It is better to use even the smallest courage, than only speak about the greatest courage that was never used. It is better to use even the smallest intelligence, than only speak about the greatest intelligence that was never used. It is better to use even the smallest enlightenment, than only speak about the greatest enlightenment that was never used.

WHEN THE WORLD IS SHOOTING AT ME

Over history, the most trying times have produced the best inventions and innovations. It is during wars and tough times that humanity feels the greatest drive to succeed, because our existence is on the line. Soldiers on the battlefield fight hard and smart while under fire from the enemy's bullets and artillery. Wars have made great men and women from ordinary people. It is overcoming challenges in life that makes one a hero, not the celebration of a rich life.

A hero is made from overcoming challenges in an external environment. If you whine, slow down or succumb to the pressure and challenges in your life, you are no different than the countless others whose lives, destinies and fates were controlled by their external conditions. A challenge is an opportunity to triumph. It is not the soldier that sits comfortably in his barracks who will be named a hero, but the soldier who did something extraordinary to save the lives of his comrades and win the war. Heroes are not made during peaceful times or when you are celebrating a good life, they are made during wars and tough times. See your trials as opportunities that can make you a hero in your own life.

We have been negatively programmed to see our failures, challenges, or tough times as embarrassment, or shameful times in our lives. We are programmed to whine about and resign to those challenges and adopt them as our permanent realities. We become the product of those environments and our destiny becomes controlled by them, rather than becoming the masters of our fates. When you become the product of your environment, you have become a slave of your environment. What you call failure, divorce, debt, mental illness, and depression are your battlefields. See them as opportunities to become a hero.

THE ART OF COMPETITION

Competition is a challenge in another form. You are constantly competing against other people or situations in life. Just as other dualities in life exist, so do winners and losers or winning and losing. In the animal kingdom, when the lion is going after the gazelle, the lion is trying to win his meal while the gazelle is trying to win his life. Survival is at stake here. When it comes to human beings, the stakes are not usually that high, but competition is natural and healthy for all. So, why do we feel empathetic and sorry for people who lose? Aren't they part of the game, just as the winners are? It is impossible for everybody in this world to be a winner. If the gazelle always won, the lions would cease to exist. If you think competition is bad, then inadvertently you are saying winning is bad, because there is no winning without competition.

Challenges and competition give you the opportunity for victory.

THE HOW AND DREAMS

It is not *what* you do that determines your success, it is *how* you do it. When you live in courage, God will not put you in a weak position. The "how" could change what you are doing, because the energy of courage will not allow you to do things that put you in a weak position.

The "how" makes you live your best life now and do your best work now. It does not matter how many years you put into achieving your goals, how can you achieve success if you are still a beggar? If you are begging for favours, such as getting a job, you are no different than the beggar on the street begging for money. A beggar will never be a master of his destiny because he is at the mercy of other people's generosity. He has abandoned his kingdom and is living as a beggar in someone else's kingdom. In begging, you destroy your self-worth. There is nothing wrong with asking for help – that sometimes help gets things done. But you must do it with dignity and not see yourself as less of a person.

If you were looking for someone to represent you in some way, why would you choose someone with a negative attitude? Would you choose a master or a slave? A fearful or courageous person? A winner or a whiner? Of course, you would pick the person with the positive attitude or character. So, why would you choose to adopt any of those negative characters for yourself? What kind of employer would hire the person with the negative attitude or a beggar? What kind of outcomes will you get if you approach life with a negative mental state?

Many dreams die because we expect other people or circumstances to help us achieve them, instead of depending on the infinite intelligence within or God. Nobody who depends on others is truly free. You cannot have two masters – Man and God - you must choose one. Reject the thoughts of depending on others if you want to be the master of your destiny.

EVERYTHING YOU KNOW

Everything you know and every value you hold has been given to you by other people. You are literally living in someone else's world, in their values system. Then you become frustrated in analyzing those values and try to understand how you fit into them. You waste your energy worrying about not living up to those values, which leaves you feeling worthless. Do you see where your deprived self-image is coming from? You have forgotten your own true worth because you feel you did not measure up to other people's expectations. Society's values change over time anyways, so do not waste your life trying to conform to the current version that is expected of you.

You are not checking the boxes you are programmed to check, so now you feel like a failure. Stop the judgement and put down the ruler that the corrupt program gave you. You have one life to live, so be true to yourself. Open your spiritual ear and listen to your inner callings.

Enoch Mamo

ENERGY

THE POISON LAW

If you swallow or drink a poison, it does not matter in whose body, stomach, esophagus, blood stream or cells it travels, it will destroy the body and kill the person. That is the same for negative energies and thoughts such as hate, fear, shame, and worry. They will destroy anybody who internalizes them. They are indiscriminate, impersonal, and impartial. The type of energy you take in is going to affect your success or failure, your health, and your peace of mind. So, what are you putting into your body? What are you pouring into your spiritual glass? Stop blaming the glass for the type of liquid it contains, ask who filled it and what is inside. Stop blaming your face or skin color. Stop looking for the answer in the ego, or from other people. Look at the energy within you - that is where the answer is.

Just like you should be careful of the food you eat; you should be careful of the spiritual energy you take in. Perhaps even more so since energy has a greater effect on your life than food. The repercussions of negative energy have a greater influence on all facets of your life. If you have been feeding on negative or junk spiritual energy, it will show in your body weight, your level of success, your joy, your health, and peace of mind. Everyday, just like food, you feed on spiritual energy. Spiritual enlightenment or consciousness will help you choose the healthy and positive spiritual intake or diet, so that you can live a happy, abundant, and serene life.

Your energy determines the condition of your life, not the other way around. The seeds you choose to sow determine the type of fruit you will be able to harvest.

If you believe in the power and truth of energy, then you will not allow any external environment, circumstances, or experiences to waste your days. If wealth and fame determined positive energy, then no wealthy or famous person would ever commit suicide. When you understand that you are energy, you can start living in the present moment. No external influence can increase or decrease the value of your energy, only your ignorance veils the value of your energy. If you believe you lack positive energy, then you will not see it.

You can not turn negative energy (something done in a negative context) into a positive product (outcome), just as you cannot turn positive energy (something done with courage and a righteousness self-image) into a negative product or outcome. No one can fail you; it depends only on your energy. You are determining the outcome of your journey right now in your own mind - before you even start doing anything. There is only one thing that determines the outcome of your projects, and that is the "how" – that is, the type of energy you carry into whatever you do, whether it is positive or negative. This is karma yoga. Nothing in this world can stop you if you get the "how" right, and nothing in this world can give you success if you get the "how" wrong. Only a fool is worried about the results. When you focus on the "how," you are living in the energy of the present moment.

THE DEVIL'S MESSENGER

There are people in this world who have unwittingly became devil's messengers and they are being used by the evil spirit to destroy the lives of other people. They destroy the great potential and creativity of other people through physical, emotional, or verbal abuse. These messengers are not aware that they are being used to bring destruction, death, failure, and misery to other people. They are the weak links - the carriers and transmitters of the negative energy in the world. Do not be sucked in. Do not judge them, or dwell on their actions, opinions or words and unwittingly become a messenger of the devil yourself by hating them. Always forgive them, for they do not know what they are doing. You have only one life on this earth, do not spend it serving the devil. Be an agent of God - of love, prosperity, abundance, forgiveness, creativity, talent, laughter, joy, peace, growth, and healing.

How can you not forgive and show compassion to devil's agents when they are already living in slavery? Help them in any way you can to set them free. There is no neutrality here – you must pick sides. You either choose to live with God or do the devil's work.

UNFORGIVENESS

We are usually blind to the sickness in others and find it difficult to forgive them when they cause us inconveniences or financial loss. We become angry and vengeful and plan revenge, instead of realizing their weakness and forgiving them. They do not mean to target you personally and they are not out to get you. They are who they have been all along. You are asking them to give you what they do not have. Can you ask a penniless man to lend you money? It is the same for people who are filled with negative energy, emotions, and thoughts. They can only give you what they have.

Even though you cannot change them, you must not allow them to change you. Do not let them make you behave or act in away that is inconsistent with your personal principles and philosophies. If you have been a loving and forgiving person, continue to be so. The blue sky never changes its color because of the dark cloud. Falling under their influence makes you a slave of the other person, which means you are living a reactionary life instead of being proactive.

Why do we believe that some sins are unforgivable? All sins are sins, borne out of ignorance, which is like a disease from which you can be cured. If a hateful person makes you hate them back, then they have passed on the disease to you. Do not allow yourself to be infected like that.

SHAME

When you live in shame, you cannot expect that negative energy to produce a positive outcome. The shame you harbour will only breed more negative emotions and thoughts. Living in shame is suffering, and who will give you back the time you wasted on shame? Nobody in this world can bring back the years or days you lost. Shame is a disease of the mind that has been created by the illusions of the ego. Guilt, regret, hate, anger, and worry are like parasites of the spirit that can destroy your life. And nobody benefits from a wasted life. How can you move forward with that kind of heaviness? What can you achieve when carrying that kind of baggage?

If you are suffering from shame, perhaps it is because of your desperation to have the approval of others. This dependence or enslavement leads you to a feeling of shame and worry. Do not waste your time or energy trying to fight shame. Instead, remove the source and the source is your desperation to create a positive opinion of yourself in other people's mind. You can use the same strategy to remove other negative emotions or thoughts, such as regret. The problem is not in what has happened in the past, it is how you feel about those things. And the only person who can control or change those feelings is you.

11

Life's Journey And Goals

LIFE IS A JOURNEY

I have always believed that life is a journey (it is continuous). What this means for me is that I live for the journey, not for specific moments. The paradigm shift of valuing the journey itself, including the everyday hustle and grind, can boost your energy and give you sustained and consistent focus on what you are doing. I see the journey as sacred, not the destination. Looking back, I remember many moments and destinations that I looked forward to in great anticipation, but those moments came and went, and they didn't last long. I then immediately shifted my focus to another destination or goal that would make me happy. I kept living for destinations.

For many, their dreams are actually nightmares, because they are living for tomorrow while wasting their present life - the now. All things in the present are better now, not tomorrow or in the future. How can you live for tomorrow? How can you dream of better health? A bigger smile? Better looks? More respect? More power? Who promised you tomorrow, anyway?

In Stephen Covey's book called, "The 7 Habits of Highly Successful People," he recommends people imagine what they would like their friends, families, and relatives to say at their funeral, and then live accordingly. I could not disagree more with this idea. It is like recommending people be slaves of other people's opinions. You should not want people to say good things about you or see you as the "good" boy or girl, just so you can live between those lines. If you break yourself to meet people's expectations, your life becomes a ransom.

SPIRITUAL JOURNEY

The spiritual life or journey does not happen in a straight line. Instead, it has its highs and lows, as shown below.

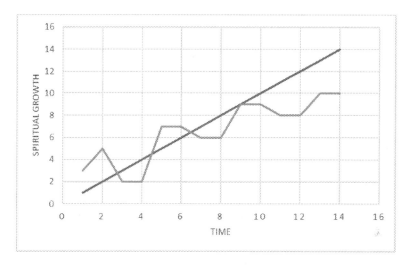

As you can see in this simple graph, some of the troughs show growth. When you feel low, remember that this year's low is still better than previous lows. And sometimes this year's lows are better than previous highs. This year's ignorance is sometimes better than last year's enlightenment. So, don't be disenchanted by the lows, there are expected in the natural progression of our journey in this life.

ENTREPRENEURSHIP

Over the past 20 years, entrepreneur and businessman Elon Musk has built more than 10 companies with a combined value of billions of dollars. This, while many others did not even change companies in the same amount of time – settling instead for mediocre productivity and earnings. How did Musk do this? It did not happen in a vacuum. The most important assets he had in achieving success were his time, mental energy, and discipline to focus on his projects. These are three assets that everybody has. We all have time, mental energy, and the ability to be disciplined, but the difference is how we use these valuable resources. Musk could also have had mediocre productivity and earnings, had he not been disciplined or spent his mental energy and time on trivial pursuits such as excessive drinking, video games or doing drugs. Nor if he spent his time gossiping about people, sports, or politics or if he gave in to the feelings of fear, anxiety and anger or hate he undoubtedly felt, just like the rest of us. All of these things were competing for his time and energy, but he chose to live a consciously disciplined life and to instead focus his time and energy to build these companies. If you cut out the excess things in your life that are stealing your energy, you will find you have more time to achieve your goals. So, Mr. Busybody, stop the confusion and focus on something worthwhile, to improve your mental, physical, and financial health. You always have the choice - to choose what kind of life you want to have and what kind of project or company you want to build.

All the immortal souls who have advanced humanity in their respective fields, had choices between right and wrong, strength and weakness, negative and positive. Every single day and hour, they had to make a choice. They did not only face positive choices; they also had the temptation to choose the negative. It is the culmination of those positive choices that led to astronomical success.

What are your days, hours, minutes filled with? What type of thoughts and actions? Look at them, you will be able to know the monetary value of your time based on those things. Will you get paid for what you are thinking, your dwelling thoughts and actions? If you want wealth and great success, then live according to your prayers.

WHENEVER YOU ARE READY

When you are ready for something, your whole being will tell you, "it is time." You will find yourself where you are supposed to be in your life at exactly the right time, because of the journeys you have undertaken. Do you think it was by chance Elon Musk was where he was at that young age? No. The people who are ready to be there will be there, because of the spiritual, mental energy and discipline they undertook to be there at that time. For Musk, no other place was ready for him but where he ended up – whether it was starting SpaceX, SolarCity, or going to Tesla at an early stage of the company's creation. Why was it not somebody else who got to occupy those roles? This is because Musk was not brought there by chance. He spent his mental energy and time preparing for those roles. This is to say, the way in which you are spending your mental energy and time now, is preparing you for roles to which you will be suitable – whenever you are ready. When it happens, you will feel you were meant to be there.

Just like travelling to physical locations, your final destination depends on the direction and speed of your journey. If you stop to rest in other cities (roles), and lose focus through worry, self-doubt or discontent, you will not make it to your final goal, or destination or perhaps you will be delayed in getting there. At whatever point you are in your journey, you were taken to that moment because of the way in which you used your resources up to that point. It was not by luck, but the accumulation of all your thoughts and actions.

A MOMENT IN TIME

It is very difficult to do anything great if you keep worrying about the long term or the future. Sometimes, I also make the same mistake about what is supposed to be important. For example, when I get a good vibe in the present moment, I tend to think, "But this is for but a moment, it will not last." Or, "How is this going to change my life in the long run? Will this have any monetary gain for me?" These thoughts and feelings devalue and dismiss the moment as fleeting. But life is made up of mere moments. Ignore or waste the moment and you will ignore and waste your life. This doesn't mean you should try and sustain those moments – just let them come and go, for however long they last. For you do not know what the next moment will bring – it could be positive or negative. Things happen and occupy you in their moment, so you cannot ignore them as if they are not happening. Do not think of their implications or sustainability, because the future is an illusion of the ego. Once the future arrives and becomes the present moment, the ego will tell you once again to waste it for another future, and that vicious cycle will waste your whole life. This moment does not need to be compared to previous ones, this identity or perception does not need to be judged against past identities and perceptions. Always trying to be someone or something else is not honoring the present moment. Accept who you are now in your present life.

STRUGGLES ARE NOT A WASTE

"Few things are more sinful than the wastage of your days for a better tomorrow." That is a quote from my first book entitled, "The Truth Shall Set You Free." It means that the time you spend struggling to get out of your challenges, failures and ignorance is not in vain. It only becomes wasteful if you see it as such, or if you spend your time feeling like a victim of your circumstance. But if you see your struggling days as an opportunity to use your courage to enlighten yourself, to gain abundance, then those struggling days become the best days of your life. You do not have to only tolerate difficulties in your life, you can thrive on those days and enjoy each moment. You will transmute all your challenges into opportunities. You will grow stronger and wiser each day. But if you see those days of challenge as a waste, it will lead you into feelings of failure and doubt. You will grow impatient as you wait for the struggles to pass, which postpones your happiness and success into the future. You will fall for the illusion of the changing face.

CLARITY IN PURPOSE AND GOALS

Your purpose or goals in life must be very clear and specific. A lack of clarity is chaos. What kind of program or software will you create by writing unclear and chaotic codes (guess work or an unplanned life)? You must write the right codes in order to use the program or software you desire.

That is the same for your future goals and daily life.

It is even more important than achieving the goals themselves, since these clear plans determine the kind of journey you will have. Make very clear goals, then you will start enjoying the music. It does not matter if you reach your destination or not, but at least you will have the clarity to enjoy life. Living a life without a plan will lead to failure, regardless of what you are doing or how busy you are. Part of your game plane must include goals you wish to achieve, and the principles and philosophies to live by.

Have you ever played a chess game without rules? It is aimless and boring. It was my son who first taught me to play chess and he is very competitive. But when I play with my daughter who is much younger, we follow no rules. Any move is a good one and I play just to make her happy. But it is somewhat boring. If you do not have a game plan in your life, your life will also be boring and aimless. You will be thrown in different directions by changing events, friends, or other circumstances. No matter how many times you failed before, you must always have a game plan for the future.

WHEN TIME BECOMES YOUR ENEMY

You will hear a lot of people saying that they are bored and do not know what to do with their time. If you have not found what you love to do in your life, then you will easily become bored. You will find many ways to waste your time by filling it up with meaningless activities such as chatting, shopping, TV, social media, and video games. But still, time looks like an endless pit to fill and they still feel bored and unimaginative. Many people gave up finding what they love, because of finances, their status, or other people's opinions.

You must be careful of people who do not know what to do with their time. They may end up wasting your time as well, while you are trying to work hard to achieve your goals. Many people do not know what to do with their time when it is not dictated to them by institutions and organizations. These people live a very repetitive life. Their dreary routines make their brain operate on autopilot most of the time. They do not want to learn new things or read about new ideas. So, how can you waste your time arguing with such people? Do not allow them to distract you from your own purpose and lose your creativity. They do not mind wasting your time and peace of mind, because they do not need peace of mind or creative thinking in their lives. Do not stoop to their level in the mud, it is too low and ugly.

WHAT IS AT STAKE?

If you are not fighting for something in life, then your life is not exciting or thrilling. It is a safe, secure life of employment and pension. There was once a soccer game between England and Belgium for a third-place spot at the World Cup. I was not interested in watching since they were not playing to win the cup. Similarly, what you play or live for determines the level of excitement and thrill you will find in your work. If you are working only to save money or to ensure job security, the level of excitement is expected to be low.

When you dedicate your life to something, it becomes your purpose and motivates you every day. Some people dedicate their lives to gaining and maintaining a house, to buying the perfect car or a private jet. Dedication can also be to a certain corporation, to athletics, music, or philosophy. What you chose to focus your life on becomes your purpose and source of income.

THE WRONG DECISIONS AND CHOICES

I am speaking philosophically here; I believe there is no wrong decision or answer. Nobody deliberately makes the wrong decision or gives the wrong answer (think of responses given during an exam or job interview). Like many others, I have made many wrong decisions in my life. But in those moments, they were all the best decisions I could have made at that time. So, if those were the best decisions I could have made at the time, how can they be wrong now? This is where you find the problems:

1. Those were yesterday's or past decisions, but today you have matured - mentally, spiritually, and emotionally. Now, you are wiser and more enlightened, so you are judging those past decisions with a different mindset or level of consciousness.

2. Who is the judge? In the past, you made the best decisions you could. But later, maybe you or someone else sees those decisions as wrong because of a different level of consciousness or value system. Perhaps you believe the decisions to be wrong because they did not result in monetary or status gain, or perhaps the decisions led to the deterioration of your mental, physical, or spiritual health. But remember, they were still the best decisions you could have made at the time, to the best of your abilities, even if they did not meet societal or external expectations. If you gave an answer to the best of your ability during an exam, what you believed to be the right choice, should you be faulted for not doing your best if the teachers mark it wrong? Yes, and No. Yes, because you should have known better or studied harder. But no - because

that was your best answer at the time. We cannot punish people for doing their best.

3. People forget to consider the internal and external factors that led you to making those "wrong" decisions in those moments.

Some of the internal factors are:

- Your state of mind - whether you were happy, sad, angry, calm, nervous or confused at the time you made the decision.
- Your health – if you felt any pain, anxiety, worry or fear. Even the kind of chemicals that were being produced in your body.
- Your age

Some of the external factors are:

- Peer pressure
- Political and economic environment
- Societal values and norms
- The level of civilization and technological growth
- Social justice and human rights
- Your level of income and marital status
- Your culture, religion, secular laws and trends or fashions

- Media such as TV, social media, and print media
- Your friend and family networks

The combination of external circumstances and internal factors influence your decisions or choices in each moment. Later, one or many of the circumstances will have changed, so you may see your past decisions as wrong.

We all make decisions to the best of our level of enlightenment, along with the internal and external conditions in which we are existing. But the most important factor is the level of your enlightenment. That is, your spiritual and mental growth. You make the best decision based on the information or wisdom you have at the time, along with the level of immersion you have had in that knowledge or information. So, do not look back. Have no regrets, fear, guilt, or shame over your past decisions.

Similarly, do not forget to accord the same level of understanding to those people who have also committed wrongs in life – especially if they have wronged you. They also did their best in those moments. Do not take it personally. In fact, this knowledge is the basis of forgiveness.

Mental Creations

12

TELEPORTING AND SIMULATION

Philosophically, I believe that simulation is a pathway on which you teleport yourself into a different version of yourself or your existence. Simulation is a means through which you send that specific information that you consciously or subconsciously want to appear on another screen as your reality. The screens are created by you in the present moment. This is the image or perception you have of yourself in the present moment. You can pull out old screens (self-images) and make one of those your current reality, or you can choose a different self-image by creating a new screen in the present moment.

You can create or pullout or replace new screens thousands of times, but the dominant thoughts and self image will win at the end and become your reality. I believe that it takes no time at all for your chosen screen to become your reality in the spiritual world. This is why I say you must believe as if it has happened.

Preparing yourself through simulation is one of the best ways of manifesting your dreams. Imagine if a doctor did not train on cadavers to learn how to do surgery, but rather simply read books and then began operating on patients? If you do not simulate your goals, your dreams will not become reality. Imagine pilots were not required to train in flight simulators, but began flying after only studying flight books? The chance of successful flight is very low. That is what will happen to your dreams without simulation, they will likely crash or never get off the ground in the first place.

Simulation saves you a lot of energy and time, as you can work through all the details of your dreams, goals, and purpose in your mind. You can visualize every component of your life without having to learn from your mistakes after it is too late.

FROM AFFIRMATION TO VISUALIZATION

Your dreams, purpose or visions can only live in you, not in anyone else. Not in your lovers or haters, your family or friends, or the people you hope to promote you, or give you a break. Nobody can visualize on your behalf. Your dreams are your own, so cherish them, protect them, and nurture them. You visualize your dreams - they do not come to you randomly. You go to them and open their boxes to see what is inside. Opening a box means creating a mental picture of what you want to see happen in your life, so that you can analyze your ideas and understand them better to see how they can work in real life.

REFORMING GOD

The impossible is trying to reform God or trying to reverse the natural laws. Knowing what is possible and what is impossible will save you a lot of time and energy. Always, the first creation is the invisible creation. This is where you apply your faith and wisdom and where you should focus your energy and time. This is where you apply imagination, visualization, and simulation. Knowing what can be changed and what cannot be changed is wisdom. The two levels of creations - the invisible and the visible - never stop. It is not like you became enlightened, faithful, or wise and then you start creating. No. You have been creating all your life, even when you were ignorant and full of illusions. The difference in enlightenment is that now you have the ability to create consciously. Consciousness is the wise use of the pre-existing power; it is not the creation of a new power. You had power even when you were ignorant, but you have been subconsciously using that power to create a life of scarcity and bad health. With enlightenment, you create abundance, happiness, and good health.

CREATION AND MANIFESTATION

Creation is in your power, but manifestation is not. You create in your invisible world and then your creations will manifest. Creating is like jumping from a tower, while the manifestation is what happens after you jump. You do not control whether you live or die. Creating is the conscious or subconscious choice from your dwelling thoughts or faith. The manifestation (what you see or witness in your visible reality) is not in your control.

If you dwelt on scarcity, then you will manifest scarcity in your life. There is no way to dwell on scarcity and manifest abundance and vice versa. The problem begins when frustrated people lose hope with the current negative manifestations in their lives. This will only multiply the scarcity. You are the author of your own life. Do not be surprised at the book when you wrote the manuscript. If you want a better life, write another one for yourself.

If an architect does a poor job designing a building, he cannot spend the rest of his life beating himself up over it. He will move on to the next project and improve his designs the next time around. In life, failure is the manifestation of a poor design by you. Many people become stuck in these results and cannot move on, such that they cannot create new projects, realities or new invisible creations for their lives. But the enlightened move on to design new and better versions of themselves - a new self-image, a new identity, a new reality, a new attitude, a new perception, or a new faith.

The egoistic mind tries to make you live in your past failures, which were the results of your past illusions and ignorance. They are just consequences that you have no control over. Those things happened because of how you used to think and live, in illusion and ignorance. Those consequences were first created in your invisible creation or world, and then manifested into your life. You have the power and control. Create a better future in your invisible world now, for you and for others. Live smarter. Worrying and thinking about the past is not a smart thing to do.

Fear, Worry And Courage

13

HOW FEAR CAME ABOUT

Fears are sometimes instilled in us from childhood, through bullying, intimidation, scolding and other forms of abuse by the adults or peers in our lives. Fear is often used to make children conform, by breaking down behaviours until the child is "disciplined", or respectful and good. The goal is a child who follows orders, rules, and instructions. Later, in adulthood, we consider fear to be a part of our nature. We forget what it is to be fearless. The idea of being confident or courageous seems alien to us. We forget what made us fearful and that we were not born that way. Fear is not actually a part of our nature. Our nature is courage and it has never left us - it was only veiled temporarily by the abuses of the past. As adults, we sometimes revert to acting like a "good" boy or girl, as we did in our past.

In the United Kingdom, the church of England, the

Clewer Initiative and the Catholic Church launched an app that enables users to report modern slave workers that may be working in the car wash industry. One of the main criteria to identify a slave worker was to look for fearful workers. The other two criteria were to try and see if the workers lived on-site and if they had inadequate personal protective equipment for their work.

When you live in fear, you become the "good" boy or girl who becomes a slave to other people's opinion and approvals. You hesitate to express feelings or opinions to avoid offending others. You want to look good in the eyes of others, and fear giving orders or taking leadership. You find ways to be controlled or dependent on others, while belittling yourself.

As we were taught fear as children, we were separated from the infinite intelligence within us. This made us forget the many abundant blessings we were born with, and we started believing we were limited, timid, or not good enough to even know what is good for us in our own lives. We were taught to doubt ourselves and our decisions.

Another unfortunate outcome of trying to be "good" is the affect it can have on the relationships in your life, including marriage. Many husbands and wives tolerate abuse in marriage and when this happens, your true potential and courage are quashed.

FEAR INHIBITS YOUR INTELLIGENCE

Fear inhibits your intelligence and creates a disability of the mind, to the point where it is impossible to make any smart decisions in life. Fear does not just come out of nowhere; it can come from someone you care about such as a boss or loved one, or from external influences such as your career or material possessions. You may experience fear when working on a project, planning a goal, or fulfilling your life's purpose. Once fear enters your mind, you lose the things or people you were trying to nurture in the first place. What you feared will come to pass.

Courageous people have not allowed fear to incapacitate their brain or thinking ability. Because they have the ability to make smart decisions without fear, they live a life of happiness, success, and good health. This is because their decisions are not motivated by fear, as they are in the case of cowards.

NOT HIDING FEAR BUT HIDING COURAGE

I once grew my hair long and left it messy deliberately to remind myself of my commitment to my purpose.

But when I looked at my face, I worried, "Is this to hide my fear? Is that why many rebels grow their hair?" But then I remembered you cannot hide fear if it is not real. If it is not part of your nature, it is not a part of your true self and the infinite intelligence within you? All these years I have been ignorantly thinking that fear is something inside me that I should be hiding. The truth is the reverse of that; there is no fear in me that I am trying to hide, there is only courage in me. And courage is what I was really hiding whenever I thought of fear. Never hide your courage and confidence again. They are truly part of your nature – the nature of infinite intelligence within all of us.

You are hiding your courage whenever you doubt yourself or hesitate to take on a challenge for fear of failure. We are all born with courage, and those who hide it more often, show fear more often. Fear is nothing but the hiding of your courage, and the events and people in your life are providing you with the opportunity to hide your courage, or not hide it.

FEAR MONGERING

The ego is very good at fear mongering - making you worry about potential issues that have not taken place yet. This is the worst kind of fear because it is a clear illusion, taking place only in your mind. It is also dangerous because, as you dwell on it and it becomes your invisible creation, it will manifest and come to pass as your reality.

It is more dangerous to have the fear of getting attacked by a lion, than facing the lion itself. Every time these illusions of fears come to your mind, ask yourself, "Is this lion in front of me?" That question should bring you back to reality and into the present moment. Use your five senses to come back into the present moment. Remember how many times and how many years these illusions of fear have wasted your life. You have had hundreds of these illusions in the past, and almost all of them came and left without materializing. Remind yourself that this is the wandering away of the mind and do not be fooled by the illusions. Go easy on yourself and be at peace with the impure thoughts. Forgive and defend yourself, and you will find that most people and the world will forgive and defend you. Attack yourself and you will find that most people will attack.

Often, we preach the idea of tolerance, but do not apply it to ourselves. When you hear your inner negative voice, do not try to silence it. Simply observe it and ignore. Focus on your positive dwelling thoughts and move on.

FEAR OF DISTURBING THE PEACE

A fearful heart is always afraid of losing or disturbing the peace. It is strange, but true. What kind of peace can you have with a fearful heart? It is always in a state of non-peace - always afraid of confrontation, facing the truth, standing up for itself or offending others. It is the same as a poor man being afraid of losing the few possessions that he has.

Peace, abundance, and intelligence live only in an audacious or courageous heart. I do not want peace if it is founded on fear.

WHAT ARE YOU AFRAID OF?

Are you afraid of living a poor life? Of being bored, discontent, shameful or angry? Do not be afraid. Let the feelings come, open the doors, and treat them as temporary guests. You will realize that they are not as harmful as you thought. What you should be careful of is fearing them. When they come, use them as material to bring out their antibodies. Channel their opposite and positive thoughts, emotions, and actions.

Negative thoughts, emotions and experiences are sources of all my philosophical ideas. Without them, I would have nothing to write about. They are the materials with which we work every day - the sources of music, love, forgiveness, joy, abundance, and gifts. Just like faith is often only used in times of struggle, courage can only be used when you have feelings of fear or worry. You only turn to courage in times of weakness, not in times of abundance or peace. What is the point of saying "I am courageous," if you do not use your courage in times of challenge?

WHY WORRY ABOUT THE BREAD?

Why worry about the bread when you are neglecting the eater? You cannot worry about money or your career when you are neglecting, disrespecting, and abandoning the one you are trying to feed – yourself. You are not really living if you are fearful and anxious or hateful and angry. How can you abandon God for a piece of bread? What is the success you are yearning for? Why do you seek the love and opinions from others when you have not loved yourself enough? Look inside and learn to respect and revere the God within you. There is eternal treasure and abundance. That is where you will find success, even in the material world.

THE DYING FACE OF PATRICE LUMUMBA

I once watched the last video recording of Patrice Lumumba, the former Democratic Republic of the Congo freedom fighter and president. He had been captured by soldiers who had overthrown his government, with the help of Belgium and the United States. His demeanour was so calm and confident, it seemed more as if he was being escorted into a state function than in the hands of his captors. There was no fear or perturbation on his face. He was full of grace and dignity, even in face of death. This, while most people are overwhelmed by even the smallest challenges in their lives. They run before they are even chased (their spirits fleeing their bodies to beg for small favours in the time of challenge).

This world belongs to the courageous, not the smartest, the most beautiful or even the strongest. The courageous can do whatever they want with their courage - kill or heal, destroy, or create. Great works of art, proud acts of leadership and innovations in science cannot be accomplished by cowards. When you overcome your own fear, along with your self-limiting thoughts and deprived self-image, then success will come to you. Courage can transform the most ignorant and empty heads into powerful leaders, admired and worshipped by millions. At the same time, cowardice and shame has turned many highly intelligent people into powerless victims, living in deprivation. Courage can also turn cheaters and liars into admired leaders and dictators. If smart and wise people do not stand up, we will continue to suffer at the hands of dangerous dictators who have nothing but courage to carry out malicious acts.

Choose a path that enables you to express your boldness and courage, as those are more important than money or fame. Abundance and wealth will follow from those qualities anyway. There are no special skills required to express your boldness or courage. When you are bold and courageous, you release the power of the infinite intelligence within you. It aligns with the current of life and all the 60 trillion of cells within you, allowing you to become fully alive and functional. That is when the hollow pipe is completely clear and unclogged, and you are one with the infinite intelligence within.

What is intuition? It is when you make a decision that is in harmony with the natural laws and the infinite intelligence within. It is the absence of feelings such as doubt, confusion, and fear. Always follow your intuition when deciding, regardless of the repercussions.

BE SURE FOR A DAY, EACH DAY

You do not need to wait for the perfect day to be at your best. When you make excuses such as, "I am busy with other things, the time is not right, I don't feel well, I am not motivated, I have a bad boss, I don't have a partner," you are wasting your time. What do you have to lose if you start being your best today? You will only lose your doubt and fear. Walk away from the bad ghosts and limiting self-thoughts of the past, they are not your friends. Salvation is not only the acceptance of the infinite divinity in you, but it is also the courageous and fierce rejection of past negative identities and illusions formed by ignorance and mental illness.

Courage is not abstract; it can be defined. Courage is following your dreams against all odds. It is living in faith and trusting the infinite intelligence within. It is the courage to face your past failures and illusions. It is the courage to forgive and love. It is the courage to walk away from abusive relationships. Courage is doing small things everyday, rather than waiting to do one big thing in your life. We all have opportunities to be courageous everyday, we only need to recognize those moments and be grateful for them. Courage does not have a specific face, race, career, gender, or style. It is not intimidating others or being loud and obnoxious. Courage is not anger or abuse.

CERTAINTY IN NATURE'S OPERATION

Nature does not operate based on chaos or luck, there is always order and harmony in the natural world - even if they appear abstract and disorderly. That is why confident people are successful. It is not that successful people are confident. Nature needs surety, definite of purpose, conviction, courage, and faith. Then whatever you pray for, you will receive - even those things that seem impossible to others.

Even though people do not usually understand how computers work, or the code that operates their programs, they are still able to use them effectively. Each application is programmed specifically to enable us to work. There is no luck or trial and error. That is how the universe works. Whatever thoughts we put into the universe, we get them as our realities, even if we do not fully understand how that happens.

14

Masters And Slaves

ARE YOU A MASTER OR A SLAVE?

We have two types of relationships in life – we are either masters or slaves to our life's circumstances and environment. The masters know themselves as a powerful creator of their destiny and fate. They focus on what they are doing, what they did and what they are going to do. Slaves focus only on what people did to them and blame others for their failures or misfortunes. Slaves live a reactionary life as their lives are an outcome of other people's actions. Their lives were chosen for them by the same people they blame and hate.

Nothing and no one in this world can hurt you without your consent. No matter what happens out there or what they do, only you can allow negative emotions to get into your mind.

LOST TALENTS

During the time of slavery in Europe, the Americas and other parts of the world, men and women who could have been great leaders, philosophers, writers, athletes, painters, musicians, businessmen, lawyers, and professors all lived as slaves. They were denied the opportunity to use their gifts and realize their potential. They lived a miserable, poor, and painful life. Those men and women were not created as slaves by their Creator, they were enslaved by other human beings for economic exploitation. So, they came to see themselves as slaves as well - adopting the role given to them by their masters. They could not realize the infinite intelligence within them, even though they all had God within.

So, what is the current economic order exploiting people's identities? What is the modern slavery? Racism. The current society has largely benefited from the past exploitations and slavery and continues to deny opportunities to people of colour. The system has already determined their value - to work and live only as casual labourers or clerks - except for the very few who escape these categories. The exploited will continue to have their self-worth and self-image determined by the corrupt system. Just like the past slaves, they may die without discovering their true potential or utilizing their gifts, talents, and intelligence. The system has casted them to live a mediocre life, and they live as the cogs in the wheel.

One of the biggest mistakes an educated minority can do is to lower their dignity and value when doing meagre jobs. Do not value yourself according to your current job. Understand that the game was rigged, and you were exploited and robbed. Do not become a willing slave of the corrupt system. Do not expect the exploiting system to give you any opportunities on silver plater, you must organize and fight for it through civil movements. When the system decides your self-worth or value, you will only see yourself as a cleaner, security guard or taxi driver. But you don't have to wear this coat if it doesn't fit you or your dreams and aspirations. You do not have to play along. You are a child of God just as any other human being on this earth. Even though there is no justice or fairness in this system, our children and grandchildren will suffer the same fate if we do not speak up. We must leave a better world for the next generation. Consider that many white South Africans came to Canada and maintain their positions, while black South Africans must often accept lower positions than the ones they previously held. The difference is race. Many talents are being wasted because professional immigrants are not being allowed to work to their full potential.

DOMESTICATION

In Yuval Noah Harari's book "Sapiens," he talks about the suffering of domesticated animals in the section called Victim of Revolution. He tells how humans tortured animals such as sheep and cattle in order to domesticate them. The average life span of a female dairy cow is only five years, and she spends most of her life pregnant. Her calves are often taken away immediately, some are locked in a small cage to prevent their muscles from forming and making a tough steak. I felt very disgusted after I learned this and vowed never to eat a steak for the rest of my life.

In the same way as the dairy cow and her calves, we are often domesticated by corporations, institutions, and governments. The most domesticated among us are some of the corporate employees and followers of religions. Just like domesticated animals, we are submissive and disciplined to do our jobs. We are put in a small cage, mental, and we are not allowed to think outside this box. When we stop using our free thinking or creativity, just like the calf, we will not be able to grow mentally. Just like the juiciest steak, we become the best employee for the corporation, as we produce excellent quality products for consumption and profit. Like the domesticated animals, we suffer and live a miserable life in order to produce for the company. It is sad to see people preparing themselves to be domesticated by corporations through schools and universities. Then they feel inadequate if they do not fit in or produce accordingly.

Why should the calf care how juicy his flesh becomes? The farmer does not care how the calf suffered, just so he could enjoy a steak. The consumer is busy chatting or gossiping while eating the steak, which will likely be wasted and thrown in the garbage. Is the calf's life worth the suffering for just a few bites? If I was to suffer or frustrate over the opinions or approval of others (their taste) regarding my ideas or philosophies, then I am living the life of the calf. I am free, I am wild. I cannot be put into a box. I would rather take the risk of living as a wild animal in the cold and rain than be caged in a "safe" tiny box and given food and water.

The enslaved corporate workers are programmed to believe that happiness comes from expensive exotic vacations, big cars and big homes or a lifestyle of excess. They never enjoy the freedom and true independence of free thinking or creativity. Just like the muscles of the juicy calf are weak, their creative minds are weak due to lack of use.

USE OF HUMAN WEAKNESS

A lot of dictators and bullies use human weakness as a major asset, and they exploit these weaknesses to their advantage. When you have no fear, no bully can make you a victim. The problem is a lot of "good" men and women are not in leadership positions because they are enslaved by these illusions of being "good." This is actually a coverup for cowardice. They believe they are nice people who do not want to offend others, so they leave the leadership positions to the more aggressive bullies and dictators. Important and consequential decisions in their lives end up being made by those in power.

DOMESTIC VIOLENCE

I watched a short documentary that stated, on average, three women are killed every day by their husbands in South Africa. While that is very shocking and saddening, those are just physical deaths. What about the psychological deaths? Many women and men are also dying every day psychologically due to verbal and emotional abuse. One woman said, "It doesn't get better, run while you can." That is, the abuser gets worse by the day instead of changing or reforming. Another said, "The knife attack came out of nowhere, I didn't see it coming." Just like most verbal and emotional abuse, attacks are often unexpected and come out of nowhere.

Abuse is not strength, whether it is physical, emotional, or verbal. Abuse is weakness and ignorance. Emotional and verbal abuse causes you to die slowly without bleeding. Abusers make their victims feel like failures. Their words and actions make the victims feel undeserving of anything good in life, including dignity and respect. The victims get tired of fighting or trying to maintain peace because they are emotionally bankrupt and psychologically dead. After years of conditioning, the victims come to believe they could not survive without their abusive partners and are overwhelmed by feelings of inadequacy.

15

Opinions And Values

TRYING TO LOOK GOOD FOR OPINIONS

One of the biggest causes of mental slavery is our attempt or desperation to try to look good to others. We do speak and act with the hopes of making them like us or looking good in their eyes. If you stop caring about their opinion, you can stop your attempts to impress them. Therefore, the control and the responsibility are with you.

CONTROLLING OTHER PEOPLE'S IMAGINATIONS

You have no right over what other people imagine or think of you. In fact, it is their right to have a very negative view of you. The issue is not their views, it is your worry about it that leads to wasting your time and energy responding or reacting to those opinions. What was enslaving you was not their opinions, but rather your need to receive a positive affirmation from them. You can solve this problem by eliminating your needs and desperation for positive opinions, thus eliminating your dependence on them.

Can you imagine if we had control over the imaginations of Einstein, N. Tesla, DaVinci, Steve Jobs, A. Lincoln, N. Mandela, MLK or other immortals? We would have lived in a world that is centuries behind - dull, uncivilized, and unjust. Therefore, the same way we are not in control of the good imaginations or opinions, we are not in charge of the bad ones either. Let every man and woman imagine - that is their God-given eternal freedom and right. No other human, circumstances or institution has power over them.

Trying to argue with people who differ with you or trying to remove the layers of veils created over many years is almost impossible. Reflect on how hard it is to change some of your old perceptions. How can you then expect to change them in others?

CLINGING TO BAD GIFTS

Many people hold on to bad or negative gifts that other people gave them (or that they gave themselves). They cling to these negative gifts in the form of a negative self-image or self-limiting thoughts and keep wondering why they cannot get rid of them. Well, it does not matter to God if you chose to live like a slave or a master, because nobody can save you from your own choice. Either you die clinging to those illusions or you free yourself and have God on your side. Abandon and reject the ignorant past illusions created by old programming, and destroy the chip. Each day, dwell on positive gifts of power, strength, abundance, and good health. Gratitude is far better than abundance. Making this choice of which gifts to accept every single moment of your life is a simple, but practical philosophy.

Coveting other people's lives shows how discontent you are, and how much you despise your own. It is a life of ingratitude and scarcity. If you have chosen and accepted the negative gift, then you have veiled the blessings of God in your life. Only accept what is good in life, the thoughts that are beneficial to you to have a good life.

WHO DESERVES YOUR RESPECT?

Most of the time, you worry and get anxious because you respect the other person more than you respect yourself. This fake courtesy is a waste of time. Focus on your own work and not other people. There is no other person who deserves your respect more than you do. Whenever you respect others more than yourself, your being reacts negatively to remind you to correct the mistake (the sin against the holy spirit) and to make you stay with God. Your essence, or the energy within you, reacts negatively to remind you to respect yourself. These negative reactions manifest themselves in the form of nervousness, worry and perturbation.

Your body will tell you through your negative reactions that you have committed a mistake. It is not punishing you for your perceived mistakes or failures, but it is reminding you to get your priorities right. To put your worth, your dignity and integrity first, to have unconditional and abundant self-love and respect. Some people misconceive these negative reactions and their manifestation as a sign of punishment. It is like you put your hand on a stove, and when the pain (which is a form of warning that you should remove your hand) you instead put your other hand on the stove. This is how self-attack works.

We are not what we gain in this life. Instead, we are shaped and created by the type of energy we possess and give. You are the energy that you carry, you are not created or determined by other conditions or people in your environment. The conditions in which you are living simply bring out that energy you carry around.

SEEKING RESPECT OUTSIDE

The respect, love, fulfillment, and approval you seek from other people or from your career will always result in either disappointment or humiliation. You can only find true love, respect, and positive opinion within yourself. If you are not giving that to yourself, nobody can give it to you. People can only treat you based on how you treat yourself.

If you perceive the love and respect you are receiving is not up to your expectations, you will become miserable and will also make the other person miserable. This perception is the source of resentment, anger, grudges, fights, relationship breakdowns and blame. Nobody gains from such expectations; it will only enslave the parties involved. The true and the infinite love, and the understanding and respect is within you already.

The best time to respect and honour yourself is now. You should not only respect yourself in front of other people (whether in public or at a place of work). What kind of respect is that? When you exhibit self-respect, confidence, courage or honour for the sake of other people, it means the one you were respecting was not really you, but them – in order to get a positive opinion from them, or make them see you as someone honourable. That is a travesty. You must recognize self-respect and self-love in yourself before you recognize any respect or love that comes from other people. This is why it is said, "The greatest treasures in this world lie within us." It is this recognition, understanding and living according to this natural law that gives you access to this treasure within. It was a lack of self-respect and love that made you think that you could not do better.

Just like love is the greatest shield you can have against external attacks or hate; self respect is the greatest source of honour you can give to yourself. The respect and dignity other people give you is temporary, because they can withdraw their respect if they feel there is no benefit to them, or if you have done something they think is not right. You will feel betrayed and valueless, which will then make you become angry and bitter because the ephemeral respect is gone.

THE SMOKE SCREEN

Many of the pleasures people seek are not sources of happiness, but sources of misery, shame, regret and hurt. The fake happiness is the smoke screen, but when you wipe the mirror, you see the negative emotions and outcomes beneath. The drug addicts began using drugs to be happy but ended up becoming enslaved. What they thought would give them pleasure turned into a monster that consumed their dignity, independence, and good health. They separated from God. Many others, even those with good jobs and great success, have succumbed to other monsters, in the form of alcohol or poor diet.

For the wicked, every opportunity is a chance to separate from God. So, it is not surprising that they would use alcohol or drugs to plunge into disgrace in the name of pleasure. It is not necessarily that alcohol or drugs always lead to a separation from God, but more that the wicked man or woman turns them into wickedness. By losing self-control you are separating from power and strengthening the muscles of weakness and indignity. All your attempts to become happy instead increase your misery, weakness, and poverty. Despite looking for happiness in those things, there is none to be found.

Indulging in leisure activities that harm your health shows a lack of conscious living. Every single second, the trillions of cells in your body are working hard to keep you alive. Your heart pumps blood to every fibre of your body to make sure it is oxygenated. Your cells are constantly replacing the dead ones to keep you healthy. Then, you deliberately harm these cells and incapacitate their functioning through excessive alcohol, smoking, drug use, bad diet, and lack of exercise. When you are under the yoke of decadence, you become a slave to its urges, you become weak and wicked. It is a force with its own power. If decadence is still the source of your happiness, you risk becoming its slave. Everyone starts as a servant, indulging in insobriety occasionally for entertainment. But slowly, its power can make you a slave. Do not try to justify your decadence, it is not your friend. It is here to take your soul.

You cannot quit such habits if you continue living in the same environment that made you sick in the first place. You will have a recurring problem. Remove yourself from the toxic environment and relationships, then seek treatment.

16

Forgiviness And Judgement

MISSING OUT ON BLESSINGS

The fights, hate, vengeance and anger we have towards other people who did us wrong make us miss out on the infinite blessings of God. If we truly believe in the presence of infinite blessings and infinite power of God to give us a good and a happy life, how can you simultaneously believe others can steal those blessings? If you believe in God, then nobody can take away what is truly yours, especially the abundance that God has given you. The theft is only possible if you believe your blessings can be stolen. When you believe others have the power to steal your blessings, you are giving them the power to do just that. Stop giving power over yourself to people who do not deserve it. No one can really hurt you without your consent, but we give consent subconsciously through fear, anger, and jealousy.

When you attack someone, you will be rattled and

angered by them. They are then in control of you and your mind; thus, you are left weakened, restless, and confused.

SELECTIVE COURAGE AND FORGIVENESS

Many of us make the mistake of being selective about what we should forgive and what we should not. You are not truly forgiving if you choose who and what to forgive. You must forgive all people, no matter what they did to you or others.

Courage is not about fighting but facing your own fears and worries. It is overcoming what has been holding you back. You must strengthen the muscles of courage by nurturing it every day, not only at certain times in your life. Observe what is happening in your life today and apply courage. Some people live in cowardice because they believe that their current condition does not call for courage but following your heart and living according to your aspirations takes courage daily. Facing and overcoming thoughts of limitation and fear takes courage all the time. Choosing to forgive, to trust, or to believe in yourself is a 24-hour job. Waiting to be courageous means you are currently living in fear, and fear can only produce more fear and misery.

TRUE GIFT, LOVE AND FORGIVENESS

True love is the love you give to those who cannot love you back or to those who hate or dislike you. Likewise, true forgiveness is what you give to those who cannot forgive you (even those looking for vengeance or trying to hurt you). All other forms of love and forgiveness are just reciprocal. They make you dependent on the actions and responses of the other person. Be a master and give love and forgiveness to others regardless of how they treated you or hurt you.

It shows lack of principle to base your love and forgiveness on the actions and reactions of other people. True forgiveness and love are natural laws. They apply to every man and every woman in this world, with no exceptions. The punishment and misery of not following these laws are eternal.

REMOVING THE LOGS FROM YOUR EYES

We usually try to remove the specks from other people's eyes before removing the logs from our own. What are the logs in our eyes? They are thoughts of doubt, discontentment, anger, and worry. They are the negative self-image and perceptions that veil the infinite intelligence within us, that clog the hollow pipe. Stop looking at others and think about the veils you haven't removed from your own life before you start pointing fingers. Judgement is an attack. We think that when we are judging, we are not losing. But that is not true. When we judge, we are losing mental energy and time, when we still have logs to remove from our own eyes.

When you think of the hurtful things others have done to you, those are the weaknesses of those people (manifestation of their dark mutants). Your judgemental thoughts about them are worse than what they did to you. Each time you give those things your thoughts, you are drinking poison, so it is you who suffers in the end. Every time you think of the other person's weaknesses, you are covering your own heart with darkness, putting out the light on your own heart. This is done in ignorance, however, so forgive yourself if necessary.

Abundant forgiveness comes from abundant mistakes and negative thoughts, failures, and weaknesses. These lessons come to you to teach your forgiveness to yourself and others. When a person hurts you, you can turn it into an opportunity for forgiveness, or a monster that haunts and consumes your life. One of the easiest ways to gain success, happiness and good health in life is through forgiveness. This is the hard job of loving yourself.

The habit and the mindset of forgiveness gives you the courage to initiate plans, meet new people or set important goals. When you approach these instances without the fear of guilt or regret, you are always ready to forgive yourself and move on in the case of failure. Imagine a mind that does not know forgiveness. It would be very difficult to venture into anything new because the fear of failure would be paralysing. If things go wrong, the mind is afraid of the shame, condemnation, and judgment it will receive from itself. A mind that does not know how to forgive is a mind that lives in fear.

HATE

There are some universal laws that you cannot mess with because they lead to a life of bitterness and misery. Among these are hate and vengeance. These two can destroy your life and must be avoided like a plague.

Let a woman or a man abuse you verbally, emotionally, or physically, let them hurt your family, let them steal everything you have. But no matter what they do to you, do not hate them, or hold grudges. Always forgive. Not forgiving them is a very painful, slow suicide. There are some people in the world who have enough grace to forgive the killers of their children or loved ones. What a big heart they have. You can forgive others for the petty things they do to you. Usually the actions are done out of ignorance and you cannot punish ignorance. How can you threaten to switch off the light to someone already living in darkness? Do not join them in darkness. Instead, give them light and enlighten them. There is also no point in trying to decipher what caused the action. Do not bother trying to look for answers to why they hurt you, or what their motivation was. It is not your business, and it helps nobody. You will not forgive because of X, but you will forgive if they were motivated by Y? The reasons they hurt you does not matter; it is better to simply forgive. Besides, trying to analyze someone else's motivations for ill deeds just keeps the poison in your system longer.

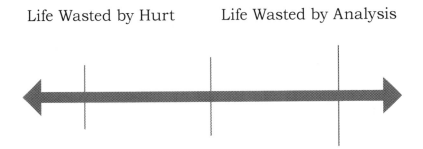

Life Wasted by Hurt   Life Wasted by Analysis

Life Wasted Due to Unforgiveness

1. Your time or life is wasted during the exposure to the hurt or abuse. This can last hours, days, or years.

2. Next, your life is wasted by the grudge you hold before you forgive. This can also last hours, days, or years. It is your choice how long this period lasts. The early you forgive the better.

3. Finally, life is wasted after during the analysis period, when you try to rationalize or investigate the hurt, its causes, and motivations. Again, you decide how long this period lasts.

On the flip side of forgiveness, is that you need not be afraid of people who do not like you. You know how devastating hate is to a life, so you understand that they are in fact hurting as well. One of the worst ways to deal with your enemy is to incite them to hate you. That will hurt them more than anything, as it will slowly kill them from inside. Hate can be used as a weapon to hurt other people because not only does it waste time and energy, it also incites emotional and physical sickness. If someone hates you, they are drinking the poison. It is very hard for you to help them, and this is a universal truth. Just stay away from them, so that they cannot physically or financially hurt you.

A lot of people are weak and ignorant, so they may dislike you from jealousy. Welcome those feelings just the way you would welcome love. It is not your responsibility to make everyone love you. If you do not have people who hate or dislike you, then perhaps you are in the role of societal slave – a "good" boy or girl who is spiritually dead.

GUILT AND PUNISHMENT

The ego looks to punish you for every small or big mistake in life. Do not fall for that illusion. No matter what kind of mistakes you commit at work or in a relationship, forgive yourself and move on. Do not listen to the ego that tries to make you fear the repercussions or punishments from others. Even if others punish you by firing you from work or ending a relationship, never make things worse by attacking yourself. You do not love yourself only when you are successful, you love yourself no matter what. You are a child of God, blessed with his love, grace and abundance. Never fear making mistakes, it is only the ego holding you back from moving forward in your life. If you can love yourself unconditionally, then the world will love you as well.

The guilty mind often calls for punishment for even the smallest things, but we are all human and make mistakes. When you stand with love, then love defeats everything. Stay with love and God will give you redemption and victories.

ROAD RAGE

Sometimes, there are drivers who will become so enraged that they are willing to start a fight or harm someone over a trivial incident on the road or in a parking lot. The best thing to do with such people is ignore their insults or hand gestures and drive away. Their rage has nothing to do with you or the incident, they are living with other issues in their lives and you happened to be in their presence for a moment. Apologize and move on. These people can harm or kill you over such stupid things and they are not worth your life, time, thoughts, or emotions. You did not plan your day for them, so do not let them interrupt your schedule.

FORGIVENESS IS THE ONLY CHOICE

I once saw a news story about two parents who were sentenced to life in prison for torturing their 12 children. What shocked me more than their actions was the children's ability to forgive. In court, the children not only said they loved and forgave their parents, one even said he was grateful for the way he was raised, because it made him who he was. Philosophically, this was a difficult, but genius choice to make. By choosing to love and forgive their parents, they let go of the anger, hate and resentment that would have wasted the remainder of their lives. That would have made their experience and whole life a complete waste. While they had every right not to forgive their parents, they also had the right to be happy, loving and at peace. Do not let the abusers in your life rob you of life. Love again and be happy again. These children reminded me of one of the greatest lessons in life, and I consider them my heroes. I wish them a great life of happiness, love, and good health.

The best vengeance you can give to your abusers is to go on to live a happy, loving and fulfilling life. This does not mean denying the abuse. If someone hurts you, you must be truthful to yourself and accept that you were hurt. But then, forgive them and move on with your life. Do not waste your time or your life analysing those dark moments. Count yourself lucky that you are free from the abuse and can now enjoy your life and love again. Every minute or hour you think of the past abuse, it is stealing another minute or hour of happiness from your current life.

17

Love

GREATEST LOVE

If one is not able to love himself, is it possible to give love to another? It is a hypocrisy to claim love for someone else when you do not love yourself. How can you claim to give what you do not have? The best sign of true love is when you treat yourself with love and respect. Love is patience, forgiveness, and respect. It is selfless and caring. And this is what you should do for yourself. No self-attack, no anger, and no guilt.

Can you imagine if President Donald Trump attacked himself for the countless mistakes and failures he went through? There would be no President Trump or billionaire Trump if he punished himself with such self-loathing. But many people attack themselves over small mistakes because they were programmed to be the "good" boy or girl, and they believe their mistakes and failures do not meet the perfect image of success set by society.

Many of the mistakes that Trump made as a politician, a businessman, a husband, or a father, could have destroyed any other man. Despite the many derogatory and hurtful things he has said and done in his life, he is still one of the richest and the most powerful men in the world, adored by his many supporters.

Love is the most powerful emotion in the world. For every day you love yourself more, you become witness to the astronomical potential of a soul nurtured by love. You must love yourself without conditions, not only when you are succeeding in life, because true love is unconditional. Those who love themselves the least receive the least love from the world. Love yourself even when you are verbally attacked (an insult is an attempt by someone to make you hate yourself). Love is your strength and power.

The love and respect you give to yourself is infinitely more important than the love and respect you get from other people. What would people do with the salt that has lost its saltiness? They would throw it out. You maintain your saltiness if you do not want to be thrown out. You do not have to wait for anyone or anything, you can do it right now and for every single minute of your life. Do not despair if you do not get love and respect from others, despair if you do not love and respect yourself. greatest love you can receive in this world is the one you give to yourself. When you love yourself like that, you will realize your saltiness or your light, and that is the time you enter your kingdom.

HAPPINESS AND LOVE

Sometimes, you may find the things you love doing are challenging and make you unhappy in the beginning. The ego tells you, "This is not for you, pick something easier. See? You failed. You are not good at it." This is like giving up on a woman that you love because she is a little difficult to get in the early days of courtship. Does this mean you should give up and settle for a loveless marriage? No. Fight for your love and make sure you get what you love out of life. Good things are not always easy but go out and get them. Do not go after easy, go after love. This is not a one-night stand, this is a marriage that you commit your whole life to.

Labour of love is not labour, but rather a source of joy and inspiration. Love overcomes everything, love always wins, love is always strong and powerful. Doing what you don't love is unimaginable torture and boredom that leads to counting the days, hours and minutes to get off work for the weekend. When you do what you love, you do not want the days to end. You can go to the end of the world for it.

RIGHT FROM WHERE YOU ARE

The secret to living your best life is to start from where you are right now. Do not wait another day for something or someone to bring you happiness. I understand some people believe they will be happy once they have a good husband or wife, or a nice home or adequate savings. They believe it is hard to be happy without having those things first, because that is the measure of happiness in the old programming. You set conditions for your happiness and the madness never stops.

So, how do you start right from where you are? Love your life, however incomplete, unsuccessful, and empty it looks at the moment. Love yourself and who you are right now. Do not set conditions to love yourself or to be happy – be here now by loving yourself. What are you building your spiritual home with? Is the foundation made from love or hate, happiness or sadness, anger or peace? Whatever you choose to build your spiritual home will determine how strong the structure is (how good or successful your life will be). Build your home block by block. It will not happen overnight, but choose the right blocks each day to continue building. Your spiritual home awaits you.

Why are challenges and failures and past mistakes

your biggest blessings? Because only a heart full of courage and forgiveness could love someone with the knowledge that all the past images were illusions. When you courageously overcome challenges and start loving yourself, you will be truly free and become a true master of your destiny and fate. Never again will everyday trivial criticisms or negative opinions steal your peace of mind or positive self-image. You should have a child-like acceptance of your life.

What is child-like acceptance here? It is the unconditional love you had for your parents and siblings. As a small child, you always wanted to be in their presence. Your family was the best family in the world, however imperfect they were. That is how you should love and accept your life; however imperfect you are. If you are denying yourself love, you are denying yourself God.

LOVE WAS PULLING ME IN

While doing my walking meditation one day, I felt like love was pulling me in, asking me, "Do you see all this beauty?" All of your experiences are like a beautiful landscape, full of mountains and valleys, forests and barren lands, green vegetation and dry yellow leaves. Nature is telling us to see it all. Only the sick eyes want to see only the green. If the whole sky were full of stars, we would not appreciate them. We are drawn and mesmerized by the stars because of their background (the dark sky). Just like your background of past failures and challenges highlight your successes to make them more beautiful.

As I write this, the date is Thursday April 25, 2019. This day will pass and will never come back, whether I spent it in happiness or sadness, in anger or peace, in love or hate. I choose how I want to spend this day. This choice is powerful and has consequences. Ally yourself with power, strength, abundance, peace of mind, and courage. The world will go on, with or without you, despite the choices you make. The world has gone on without many of the great leaders and inventors from the past, even though their contributions have had significant impacts on the modern world.

Do not hold today ransom for tomorrow, whether for money, wealth, or marital status. Do not allow the pursuit of those things to waste your day. Those things can come and go, but once this day is gone, you will never get it back.

THE WORK OF LOVE

Most people choose their careers for money, rather than love. The mind gets involved and comes up with so many reasons why you should choose this career or that field, but the heart has only one motivation, and that is love. Love is the greatest source of ideas and inventions, as there is no genius without love. You will never get true satisfaction from abandoning what you love doing in exchange for money, because you risk wasting your life envying the success of other people who are doing what they love. Nothing is going to fill the void left by love. You may try to fill this void through sex, drugs, material possessions, marriage, children, education, religion, adrenaline sports, alcohol, cigarettes and too much time on TV and social media. Instead, show yourself self-love by living according to your dreams, aspirations, and prayers. This is when you end the agony and confusion of trying to walk on two paths at the same time.

Lessons And Transmutation

18

NOT IN VAIN

I heard a story in the news one day about a mother whose young daughter had died after being left in the car all day. The mother had forgotten to take her out of the car and drop her off at daycare. In the story, she said she could never forgive herself. I was very sad to hear that. She decided to volunteer for an organization that creates awareness for parents about forgetting their kids in cars. She was trying to save lives and save other parents from going through the kind of pain and guilt she was going through. The mother said she didn't want her baby's death to be in vain. She believed if she could save even one life through her volunteer work, her baby's death, along with her own pain and suffering, would not be in vain. Hearing this woman's story increased my own resolve to continue sharing the lessons I learn from my experience. I do not want anyone else to go through the unnecessary pain and negativity

I have gone through. However small, I wanted to make my contribution teaching about courage, love, forgiveness, happiness and peace of mind.

During his psychoanalysis study, Sigmund Freud used hysterical women to study mental illness. Healthy, stable women or men were not useful for his study, just as a rich and comfortable life is not useful when studying philosophy and spirituality. My past challenges and pain have provided me with a great many resources for my study and writing. Without them, I would have nothing to write about. So, how can I despise these resources when I can use them for enlightenment and to share my lessons with others.

DO NOT GIVE EXCUSES

Do not give excuses for not living the kind of life that you wanted to live, or for not achieving your dreams. Do not blame the economy or racism or other external factors. They will not make a way forward for you - you make your own way. They do not do anything for you, you do things for yourself. Do not pay attention if people say no to you a thousand times. Above all, overcome the egoistic thoughts of feeling sorry for yourself.

The excuses you make are the best indicators about where you should work on making improvements in your life. By giving and accepting excuses in your life, you are separating from God through the recognition and acceptance of negative gifts.

Whenever you feel like giving excuses as to why you are not living your best life or full potential, stop and write down those excuses and work on them. Excuses are opportunities to help you realize where you need to make improvement. Do not become your own worst enemy and allow your excuses to determine your life.

INTERNAL POWERS

Internal powers are the powers you have within, such as the power to forgive and the power to love - even the power over your own health. Not recognizing or using these powers that have been given to you can make you feel powerless. It is like you are given constitutional rights over these powers, but you do not exercise them. It is only the weak and the wretched that see themselves as powerless and wish for other people or circumstances to give them power. They are always looking for external forces to hand them power while they ignore the power they have within.

INTRODUCING HATE

I intentionally introduced the word hate in my writing, because it fully captures a true feeling, rather than saying dislike. The opposite of hate is love. Hate comes with a lot of love's opposite energy, and there are some things that require that level of energy to sustain – such as self-pity or cowardice.

You can hate negative ideas and perceptions, but do not hate people. You can hate ignorant and criminal actions, but do not hate those who do them. The word hate comes with strong emotions, such that you would distance yourself from those things you hate. This distance will reduce the chances of you going back to those emotions, thoughts, values, and perceptions. It also makes it clear and firm where you stand regarding certain ideologies, perceptions, and values in the now. Hate comes with a powerful advantage when fighting mediocrity. It would be very difficult for you to slide back into your old beliefs, principles, and philosophies when you clearly understand what you hate and what you love. There would be no more ambiguity or doubt in where you stand. This means you can use the power of hate to your advantage.

Ignorant people, however, use hate for killing and destruction, while the wise use it for empowerment and for good. Hate is just like any other gifts of nature – they can be used for good or bad.

SELF-EVIDENT TRUTH

In the American Constitution, it is written that all men are created equal. But the founding fathers who wrote these words did not live by them or practice them in their daily lives. It took America decades, or even centuries, to begin living that truth.

Even though I try to live my life 100 percent according to the natural laws, I am but an imperfect human and a work in progress. If I fail to manifest something in my life, it is not because the laws were not true, it is because I was not able to apply them adequately in my daily life. Everyday, I work on closing that gap.

Knowing the truth is not enough to change your life or situation, you must also live by the truth. Writing about the truth that all men were created equal did not change anything for the people who were enslaved and treated as unequal. Only actions could make it true. If you do not live by the truth, then no individual or society will change.

For example, everyone knows that physical exercise is good for your health, but that knowledge does not make you healthy. Exercising makes you healthy. That is the same for all the natural laws. Who is healthier, the expert in health who does not exercise, or the man with little knowledge who exercises every day? Of course, it is the latter. It is the same with the knowledge of the natural laws. Knowing them is useless if you do not live by them.

LESSON FROM INVOLUNTARY

There was an incident involving a man who killed ten people by driving a van through a group of pedestrians. Later, it was discovered that he was angry about not having sex with women. He was a member of an involuntary celibacy group formed by men who blamed their lack of sexual activity on women. Astoundingly, he blamed his circumstances on women, and viewed himself as a victim. He became so filled with hate he was driven to commit mass murder. If only he had seen his circumstance as voluntary - a result of his actions or inactions. Maybe then he would have succeeded in becoming sexually active with not only one, but many women, if that is what he wanted. But because he saw himself as a powerless victim, he never took any steps to improve his situation and became overwhelmed by his perceptions.

If you find yourself blaming others for your current misfortunes, consider that these things happened to you voluntarily, due to your own actions or inactions. This brings the power back into your hands and gives you the choice to do something about it. You will no longer feel like a powerless victim as you will realize the situation is something you have control over.

NEVER COOKED ON ICE

I have never cooked any food by putting my pan on a block of ice. It would just make the food cold. That is because you must use heat, or fire, for cooking. Both ice and fire have different energies. So, when we try to achieve success and a good life by making ourselves slaves through fear and worry, it is like trying to cook food on ice. To cook your food (to have a good life), you need the right energy (heat). Just as ice will never cook your food, negative energy will never give you a good life. There are no surprises here. Evaluate your life to see if you are putting your pan on ice and expecting it to cook your food.

Immersion

19

KNOWLEDGE IS NOT ENOUGH

There are two 2 types of failures in life:

1. A failure because of ignorance, lack of knowledge or wisdom.

2. A failure from not acting on your wisdom, faith, and beliefs

The second kind of failure is a lack of immersion or lack of assimilating new facts and wisdoms you learnt. In this case, you know what to do, but you choose not to act because of laziness, doubt, or old programming. These kinds of failures are more painful than the first kind of failures because you know you can do better. You can only fail at immersion through your own fault. The old programming leads you to doubt, laziness and inaction, when you fall for its illusions.

KNOWLEDGE GAIN VERSES KNOWLEDGE APPLICATION

Absorbing or gaining of knowledge is a time-consuming process as you read and understand different theories or principles. But the application of that knowledge is not as time-consuming, as you can simply make it a part of your everyday life. That is what I call immersion - the knowledge becomes part of you. When you gain knowledge, it stays only in your memory, it is something you possess but not something you are. But when you apply that knowledge in your everyday life, it becomes part of you. While you can teach others the knowledge you gained, its benefit to you is very insignificant if you are not using it in your everyday life.

INTELLIGENCE AND KNOWLEDGE

I believe intelligence is the real beauty and treasure in life, while information stored in our memory is vital for our existence. Intelligence exists in the universe, while knowledge is information that lives in an individual's mind. Intelligence is the source of all imaginations and creativity and all new creations, while knowledge helps to continue the operation of those creations. Intelligence is up for grabs for anyone with good spiritual ears, while knowledge is accumulated in people's individual minds. Intelligence is thrilling and exciting, while knowledge is functional.

For example, the formula E=mc2 was not in Albert Einstein's mind or memory, it was in the universe and he wrestled it out of nature's hands. Similarly, the discovery of how to make an AC motor was not in Tesla's mind, it was already in the universe waiting for someone to grab it. All intelligence is in the universe waiting for the rightly tuned ear to snatch it up.

Intelligence is spiritual or divine. Once you have it, you must refine it - just as you polish and refine gold and diamonds to bring out their beauty. E=mc2 and other discoveries are all just polished intelligence, garnered from the universe.

WISDOM NOT USED IS LIKE MEMORY CARD

Knowledge that has not been used is as useful as information on a memory card. In this case, your brain is like a storage device, with no real use unless the knowledge is put to use. It is a waste of time to accumulate knowledge in your brain without using it to make your life, and the life of others, better. Information is not power unless you use it in your own life. A memory chip containing very powerful and important information can be lost or even thrown away - it has no power to do anything or act on its own. Information only has life when it is applied.

From the time of making simple tools to the industrial revolution, human beings have been applying knowledge to invent things and solve problems to advance society. Philosophy is no different. Every new idea in philosophy should be used to solve problems and improve lives. A person who knows the truth but does not live by it is like a drug addict who knows drugs are bad but continues abusing them.

Even the smallest action, immersion or application of knowledge is infinitely greater than tonnes of information being stored in your brain but never being used. Being alive means making a movement every single day, especially towards your goals.

It is not the man who had the information who succeeds, but rather the man who uses it. For example, the company Xerox had technological information, but failed to use it, so the company Apple acquired the information and put it to use immediately. Xerox died, and Apple is now a trillion-dollar company. The same applies when it comes to philosophical knowledge or information. If a big company with so many intelligent engineers can make such a mistake, what about a common man or woman?

We live in a day and age where the click of a mouse gives you access to all of the information you would ever need. But what we do with that access, and when, is what sets us apart from others. Information will not change your life, but information applied will. You do not even need a lot of information to succeed. As long as you use what you have wisely, the truth will set you free.

SOCCER MATCH

I watched a soccer match between Juventus and Real Madrid when star footballer Cristiano Ronaldo scored one of the greatest overhead bicycle kick goals in history. The difference between players like Ronaldo and other average players is their faith. Ronaldo and other top players have the confidence and conviction that they can score more goals, make better plays and display greater skills consistently. Players with self-doubt or who settle for mediocrity do not dream of such success. The enthusiastic search for greatness can only be activated by faith.

I have also seen Ronaldinho, another amazing

footballer, literally dance with the soccer ball, doing amazing tricks while dribbling the ball dazzlingly past his opponents. I wondered, "How can someone with such an amazing relationship with the ball not be the world's best player?" If you have the same kind of relationship with what you do, how can you not become the best in the world? That by itself is the greatest success you can have in life - enjoying the journey. Just like Ronaldinho, it is the love you have for your art or work that brings out greatness. Loving what you do will lead you to greater success in your career, and great financial rewards.

THE TWO BECOMING ONE

I have often written about the two becoming one, in terms of the infinite intelligence within and the conscious mind becoming one. While this is important, it is even more important to align your actions, habits and behaviours with your goals and dreams of who you want to become. When you fall for leisure, but dream of inspiring others, then you are the only one standing in your way. You may work hard and spend a lot of energy and time trying to achieve something, but then you allow leisure to destroy everything you have worked for. Decadence will always leave holes on the canvas of your life - holes of weakness, financial loss, and loss of purpose.

If anybody else in this world lived the way you lived, they would have realized the same levels of failure or success as you. Just like combining different chemical elements gives you different compounds (for example, two elements of hydrogen and one element of oxygen gives you a water compound), the outcome is always the same, regardless of who the scientist is.

Learn from your past failures and remove those elements of failures. Then you will realize that your success does not depend on other people's opinions nor any other external conditions, but rather on you.

Conclusion

Your own journey to spiritual enlightenment will follow its own course. To help you find your way, I have included here a summary of the main points and ideas from this book, by chapter.

FAITH

We all have faith - there is not a faithless man or woman. Even in our ignorance we still had faith that created scarcities and pain in our lives. We can all use this intrinsic power consciously and wisely to manifest abundance, good health and happiness in our lives.

SPIRITUAL MUTATION

In the normal process of our development, we adopt various inner personalities. Some of these personalities are life-enriching while others bring misery and pain into our lives. Uncovering the dark mutants or personalities will help us overcome these dark personalities, as we will stop strengthening their control and influence over our lives. When we separate ourselves from the maladaptive malignant spirits, we will also stop defending or keeping them secret.

MEASUREMENT AND PERCEPTION

As Marcus Aurelius Put said, "the happiness of your life depends upon the quality of your thoughts." How you see your life and circumstances have incredible influence on the quality of your life. You can consciously train your mind to see the positive in unfavourable circumstances and transmute them for your own benefit and enlightenment.

SOCIETAL PROGRAMMING

The realization of who we are today is a result of the values and perceptions we received from our parents, schools, religion and other institutions. This gives us a great foundation to bring changes in our lives through abandoning any harmful or backwards values in order to adopt new perceptions and values for a better life. In the past, you were a recipient of the program, now you start creating your own program.

NATURAL LAWS

Understanding the natural laws will help you draw your own personal principles and philosophies to create a better life for yourself and others. We have to learn how to realign our thoughts and actions according to these laws to meet our unique goals and challenges in life. Just like a single scientific law or principle is used to create countless products and services, natural laws are used as guidance - but not as rules - to create a uniform lifestyle for everyone.

CONTENT AND DISCONTENT

Contentment is spiritual, not material. Practicing gratitude will make you more positive in life and this will give you the right attitude to create more abundance and joy.

CONSCIOUS AND SUBCONSIOUS MIND

Understanding the interactions, limitations and power of our conscious and subconscious mind will help us live a life of self-awareness and self-control. We can train our conscious mind to unleash the power of infinite intelligence within.

SELF-IMAGE

How we see ourselves determines the level of our success and the quality of our interactions with other people. Clinging to our egoistic identity will limit our boundaries and experiences in life. Overcome your past egoistic identity and you will discover your true potential and self.

CHOOSING GOD

We can choose to realign ourselves with love, power, forgiveness, courage and the infinite intelligence that animates every living things and objects in the universe. Choosing to stay with God despite our challenging circumstances will strengthen our faith and brings forth abundant blessings in our lives.

THE HOW AND ATTITUDE

You can learn how to bring together positive energy, attitude and focus to achieve your goals. We learn how to value our time and energy by overcoming failures and rejections. We also learn how to recognize and overcome detractors and obstacles that can slow down or prevent us from achieving our goals.

LIFE'S JOURNEY AND GOALS

Appreciate the small moments in your life rather than waiting for big moments to celebrate your success. Success and failure are cumulative. Appreciating the journey will help us live in the present moment, as well as measure our progress and increase our productivity.

MENTAL CREATIONS

In mental creation, we can use simulation and visualization to achieve our goals. Understanding the power of your invisible creation will make you pay more attention to your thoughts and perception to create a good life for yourself and others.

FEAR, WORRY AND COURAGE

Understanding how we learned and acquired fear will enable us to overcome it. The detrimental effects of fear in our lives can be overcome by recognizing it for what it is - an illusion that exists only in our minds.

MASTERS AND SLAVES

Recognizing ourselves as the creators of our circumstances and fate will put the responsibilities of our lives back in our hands. This will reduce blame and a sense of victimhood. The masters have the control and power to change their circumstances and create a future of their own choice.

OPINIONS AND VALUES

Seeking and depending on the opinion of other people enslaves us. You can overcome this dependence by valuing your own opinions and values. We should neither try to control or muzzle the opinions of other people but focus on reducing our dependence on positive opinions to feed our ego.

FORGIVENESS AND JUDGEMENT

The importance of forgiveness is taught by all religions and cultures. True forgiveness is a forgiveness to all, and for all kinds of hurt anybody has caused us. Selective forgiveness is not true forgiveness. Not only does judging other people have a negative effect on our lives, it wastes the time and energy that we could have appropriated for self-improvement.

LOVE

To love other people or do good in the world, you have to love yourself first. Loving yourself is not a selfish act, but rather an act of self-respect, dignity, and a healthy sense of self-worth and integrity. This self-love will help you overcome adversities and challenges in life. It is the foundation of all success and philanthropy in this world.

LESSONS AND TRANSMUTATION

All failures, rejections and challenges in our lives can be used as lessons to make us stronger and gain new wisdoms. You can learn to transmute your adversities and how to take responsibilities in your life. Your past troubles are not all in vain, they are invaluable resource that can be used to fuel your future prosperity and good health.

IMMERSION

Understanding the natural laws or other spiritual and philosophical ideas is not enough, you have to use them to have a better life. Immersion is the moral assimilation and application of these wisdoms in your daily life. It is living according to your prayers and aspirations.